I0457028

Living In Korea

A Guide by Adoptees

Palace in Seoul, South Korea, photography by Antonia Giordano

By Adoptee Hub

A collection of firsthand experiences from adoptees living in Korea.

Volume 2: Korean Adoptee Booklet Series

Copyright and Disclaimer Notice

Seoul, Korea, photography by Antonia Giordano

3

Contents

Founder's Letter

Ami Nafzger, 2022

As the founder of G.O.A'L Korea (Global Overseas Adoptee's Link), First Secretary General of G.O.A'L (1997-2003) and the Founder & President of Adoptee Hub (April 2018 - Present) and as your fellow adoptee, adoptive parent, peer and your friend, I pledge to you that I will continue to work hard on behalf of adoptees around the world, but I ask you to join me and work together in making our community stronger. I did not build G.O.A'L and Adoptee Hub alone. This will take a village. This cannot be successful without you.

The history of international adoption started with the Korean War almost 70 years as of today. Unfortunately, there are still little to no post-adoption services to assist adoptees who visit Korea in search of their identity. Adoptee Hub was founded to fill in the gap of services, support, and resources that can help strengthen identities. I want to recognize the hundreds of volunteers from G.O.A'L and Adoptee Hub who commit their time, energy, and passion to help our community grow. They are the backbone and are amazing humans. Our volunteers have strived to provide you with a rich resource to help you navigate your way as you continue to learn about and discover Korea, a special place in our life.

Please continue to support Adoptee Hub so we can help you and your fellow adoptee peers. And as always, remember to pay it forward and be kind to others.

Ami Nafzger

President and CEO, Adoptee Hub

Dedication

This is for adoptees throughout the world. Many of us are always in search of ourselves, constructing our own identities. Some of us have a tidal wave of grief that our life started on the doorstep of a city hall in our birth country. Some of us have grown up with the concept that we were not wanted. Some of us carry a sadness within us and we learn to live with it and it persists into adulthood. Opportunities will arise and so you may choose to search and embrace the chance and learn your history, culture, and language. Whatever you do, continue searching for yourself, and know that, as with many things in life, just when you think you know yourself, another unknown door will open.

There is no blueprint for us. No one is going to save us. We need to be our own shepherds. We are the heroes we've been hoping for and we have the power to serve and help ourselves, and each other. Come join me.

Ami Nafzger
Founder, adoptee, and adoptive parent

"One lives not for oneself, but for one's community."

Ruth Bader Ginsburg, Former Associate Justice of the Supreme Court of the United States

Introduction

As a Korean adoptee, there are few guides that provide an all-in-one resource for returning to the country of your birth. (Note, use of the word Korea or Korean throughout this guide refers to the country of South Korea or people of South Korean origin.) For many, this is a pivotal step in their adoption journey. This guide was created by Korean adoptees to help their fellow adoptees plan and get the most out of this life-changing experience. It includes highlights from Korea's eight provinces, eating Korean food, traveling in Korea, daily living, and much more. You will read many insider tips sprinkled throughout this guide from adoptees who live there.

About the Korean Adoptee Booklet Series

This booklet is the second in a series aimed at providing valuable information for adoptees and their families. We hope it will be a valuable resource, whether this is your first time living in Korea or your 4th time. Look for other volumes coming soon. Other volumes will cover birth search, health and wellness as an adoptee, Korean cooking, and becoming a U.S. citizen.

For more information about visiting Korea, there is a guide also published by Adoptee Hub entitled *Visiting Korea: Volume 1.*
Visit https://adopteehub.org for more information.

Living in Korea really shaped me to become who I am today.
Learning and living with the people, and experiencing the food,
customs, traditions, and culture will always be a part of me. It is an
experience I will always treasure and never forget.

–Ami I. Nafzger, a.k.a. Jin InJa

 Adoptee Hub: Who We Are

Mission:
We exist to connect adoptees with each other; seek to collaborate with existing organizations and provide stronger services and resources that might otherwise not be available; and strive to preserve our adoption cultural legacy and community.

Connect:
We connect adoptees with family members and other adoptees through events, resources, and services.

Collaborate:
We seek to collaborate and bridge gaps left by other adoption entities to provide essential post-adoption services that do not currently exist or are not readily accessible in a system that can be difficult for adoptees to navigate.

Preserve:
We strive to preserve our adoption cultural legacy, history, and community by highlighting adoptee stories and promoting artistic talent in film and literature.

Goals:

1. In a couple years, Adoptee Hub hopes to provide translation services, counseling, support groups, cultural and language resources, as well as birth search services.
2. After our post-adoption services are in place, our goal is to hold a Global Transracial Adoptee Film Festival.
3. A larger goal of ours is to establish an Adoptee Hub Cultural Center! The center will be a bridge to serve adoptees, their families, and the greater adoption community.

Getting Involved

Membership & Partnership

- Become a supporting member
- Join our "Connect Us Program" and connect us with philanthropists or large donors you know, to help us grow our programs and services
- Join our "Partnership Program" and advance your company, while providing a 10-20% discount to our members only
- Join our "Peer to Peer Program" by fundraising for us
- Follow us, like us, share us on social media: Facebook, Twitter, Instagram, YouTube
- Spread the word about Adoptee Hub, this is a global initiative
- Attend our future events

Donate & Volunteer

- Donate goods and/or your services
- Donate to our annual silent auction
- Donate to us to support our events and programs on our website www.adopteehub.org
- Pick us as your charity on AmazonSmile.com
- Donate to us on GiveMN anytime
- Ask your company to match your donation to us
- Ask your company to pick us as their charity
- Pick us as your legacy, and add us to your will
- Pick us as your charity, and create a Facebook charity birthday event
- Dedicate "Well Wishes" to an adoptee, by donating to our program on a recurring annual basis in their name.
- Volunteer your time and help build our services and make a difference

Adoptee Hub volunteers, November 2021

Adoptee Hub 2021 annual fundraiser, photography by Kim Jackson

Contributors

Book Design:
Ami Nafzger
Aron Spiess

Cover Design:
Aron Spiess

Editors:
Amy Haggenmiller, Senior Editor
Aron Spiess
Amanda Parish
A.D. Herzel

Photographer:
Antonia Giordano

Writers:
Amanda Jackson
Amanda Parish
Ami Nafzger
Kara Dewhurst

Contributors:
Julie Hedlund
Jane Joeng Trenka
John Ha
Kate Powers
Madds Nielsen
Megan Green
Scott Adam Kaveny
Li Marie Andersson

Sponsors

Adoptee Hub is grateful to the following sponsor for their generous gifts and support of this book series.

The Hedlund Family Fund

Acknowledgements

Kamsahamnida (감사합니다)

The Hedlund Family Fund

Thank you to the Hedlund Family Fund for your generous donation. Your seed will help Adoptee Hub grow and see our endeavours to the end.

Liz, Connor, Kelsey, Doug and Julie Hedlund

Letter from the Hedlund family

Our adoption journey started as a family when our daughter, Kelsey, arrived at the Minneapolis International Airport on July 27, 1996. She was four and half months old. Little did we know at that moment how much this tiny little bundle of joy, and all that she represents, would enrich our lives, and complete our family to the extent that it has. During Kelsey's childhood, our family embraced all things Korean by attending cultural events with other adoptive families, celebrating Korean holidays, and making Korean foods. We decorated the Christmas tree with Korean ornaments, and both Kelsey and I have attempted to learn some of the Korean language, which we admit is not an easy task. The richness of Korean culture has been so interwoven into the fabric of our family at this point that we cannot imagine how we would define our family without it.

While in college, Kelsey's interest in learning more about South Korea and where she came from really peaked. In 2019, when Kelsey was 23, she and I made what we view as our first of many trips to South Korea to connect with her birth country. It was the trip of a lifetime! Over two weeks, we had the opportunity to visit Kelsey's Korean adoption agency, visit her place of birth, and see many beautiful parts of South Korea. But, most importantly, what the trip did for us was make Kelsey's history, and where she came from, real in a way that we had never experienced before. Immersing ourselves in the culture and experiencing day-to-day life helped us understand what being Korean was like and be able to appreciate that so much more. Since that trip, Kelsey has talked many times about wanting to live in South Korea and that may happen when the timing is right. If it does, her family supports her. Kelsey and I wanted to go back and visit South Korea in the summer of 2021, but COVID-19 restrictions put a stop to that. We are currently making plans to return to Korea in the summer of 2022.

Another important component of our journey has been our family's association with Adoptee Hub. We are so grateful to Ami Nafzger and all the volunteers at Adoptee Hub that give countless hours of their time to help Korean adoptees and their families connect with their Korean heritage. Our association with Adoptee Hub fills a void in Kelsey's life that her family cannot fill, and for that, we are very grateful. On behalf of the Hedlund family, it is our privilege to be able to support Adoptee Hub in the creation of this book "Living in Korea." We hope that you find it informative and that it helps you in your own journey.

Kelsey and her mother
Julie at age 2.

Kelsey and Julie Hedlund's trip to Seoul
visiting Eastern Social Welfare Society

Sincerely,

Julie Hedlund

Moving to Korea

People who have visited Korea — once, twice, or several times — often view visiting Korea and living in Korea as similar. However, through the eyes of many adoptees' lived experiences, they are quite different from each other. This book Living in Korea will help you learn and prepare you to move forward and reside in your birth country, whether for a season or for many years.

If you are thinking about moving to Korea, it can be overwhelming trying to find information relevant to a Korean adoptee. You've come to the right place! Contained in these pages are insights from Korean adoptees who have embarked on this journey and want to help make your move easier.

Whatever your reasons may be for moving, you should keep several considerations in mind as you plan your next steps.

Climate

Korea has four seasons; it is on the same latitude as the central part of the United States. Each season is distinct, ranging from a dry and snowy winter to a hot and humid summer. It is an island nation which contributes to a higher amount of humidity than you may be used to and it has many mountain ranges that affect the climate as well.

Winter in Korea

Winter is typically cold and very dry. In the cities, Korea receives less snow than in rural areas. Usually, temperatures are about 27° F (-2.78° C) and snowfall can vary, depending on where in the country you are living. Korea is known for its ondol (온돌) or heated flooring. This is a traditional Korean floor that is often used in place of standard central heating. The heated floors are comfortable and can make the room feel cozy.

Winter Holidays

Be aware that Korea celebrates some winter holidays that may impact your moving plans with business and transportation closures.

Winter in Korea, photography by Antonia Giordano

New Year's Day: Known as Sinjeong (신정), there is no special celebration. Regardless, many people will mark the occasion by making a wish and watching the first sunrise on January 1st.

Lunar New Year: This event is called Seolnal (설날). It typically takes place in February, depending on the lunar calendar. It is typically a three-day celebration and is considered a major holiday in Korea. Families gather from all over to pay respect to both ancestors and elders. Children bow to their elders and receive a small gift of money. During this holiday, many stores and restaurants will be closed and public transportation is also limited. The cities in Korea will be very quiet since people usually travel to their hometowns.

Spring in Korea

Temperatures this time of year run between 59° F and 64° F (15° C to 18° C). This is a popular time to move to Korea, as the weather is not too cold and not too hot.

> **Pro Tip: If you are a person with seasonal allergies, it is recommended to bring allergy medication and to carry this with you along with a face mask to help reduce reactions.**

Cherry blossoms in Seoul, South Korea, photography by Antonia Giordano

This is also the cherry blossom season in Korea and it is beautiful to see and smell. The first bloom is predicted to arrive in late March or early April and lasts for one to two weeks. Some areas have festivals you can attend including Cheju Island (제주도); Jinhae, Kyung Sang Province; (진해 군항제, 경상남도); Hwagae City (화개시); Gyeongju (경주시); Seoul Yeouido (서울여의도); and Daegu City (대구시). Mark your calendar and make plans to visit these places while you are living in Korea.

Spring Holidays

Children's Day: This occurs on May 5th and is considered a national holiday. This day highlights the dignity of children and their need for love, care, and respect. It is also a day to honor adults that have contributed to improving the lives of children. Children of all ages are celebrated during Children's Day and the entire community can get involved in the festivities. Many cities have parades and public activities, including free admission for kids at museums, zoos, amusement parks, and movie theatres. Traditional games, such as the popular ancient board game Yut (윷) and Nori (노리) are played. Gifts are given to children.

Pro Tip: Be cautious, the air quality is often low this time of year due to air pollution and yellow dust that comes from China. Bring face masks to wear or purchase them locally to protect yourself.

Children's Day, photography by Antonia Giordano

Buddha's Birthday: At the beginning of May, Buddha's Birthday (부처님 오신날) is celebrated and is a particularly important day for the nation's practicing Buddhists (a religious group that makes up approximately one-fifth of Korea's population). It is also a public holiday that is widely celebrated across the country. Many cities will have lantern parades and decorations around the city. Buddhist temples will also have special festivities surrounding the holiday which start about a week before the day itself. You may start seeing decorations going up a month ahead of time, including vibrantly colored lotus-shaped lanterns.

Buddha's Birthday, photography by Antonia Giordano

Summer in Korea

This season is often hot and humid. The temperatures run about 90° F to 102° F (32.2° C to 38.8° C) and the humidity can make it feel much hotter. This could make moving to a new country extremely uncomfortable and challenging. June and July bring the monsoon season where it can rain nonstop for days. The Busan area is particularly affected by these. Keep in mind, there is little central air conditioning in Korea. However smaller air units can be found in many establishments such as restaurants and coffee shops.

Summer in Busan, South Korea , photography by Antonia Giordano

Autumn in Korea

This is known as the most beautiful time to move to Korea. The daytime temperatures range from the mid 70s° F (23.9° C) to mid 80s° F (26.7° C). In the evening, the temperatures can drop into the mid 60s° F (18.3° C) and you may need a light jacket. There are few trees within the city, but there are many in rural areas with beautiful fall colors.

Fall Holiday

If moving to Korea at the end of September, be mindful that this is when Koreans celebrate Chuseok (추석), one of their biggest holidays of the year. Chuseok is equivalent to Thanksgiving and is celebrated for three straight days. Many businesses will be closed during this time, which means food, goods, and transportation may be exceedingly difficult to find.

Fall in Seoul, South Korea , photography by Antonia Giordano

Here's a complete list of holidays Korea observes:

Winter:

- 25 December – Christmas (기독탄신일 or Gidoktansinil)
- 1 January – New Year's Day (신정 or Sinjeon)
- January or February– Korean New Year (설날 or Seolnal)
  - Takes place on the second new moon after the winter solstice. The dates are adjusted every year according to the lunar calendar.
- 1 March – Independence Movement Day (삼일절 or Samiljeol)

Spring:

- 5 May – Children's Day (어린이날 or Eorininal)
- April or May– Buddha's Birthday (부처님 오신 날 or Bucheonnim Osinnal)
  - Takes place on the 8th day of the 4th lunar month. The date is adjusted every year according to the lunar calendar.

Summer:

- 6 June – Memorial Day (현충일 or Hyeonchung-il)
- 17 July – Constitution Day (제헌절 or Jeheonjeol)
- 15 August – Liberation Day (광복절 or Gwangbokjeol)

Fall:

- September or October – Chuseok or harvest day (추석)

- Takes place on the 15th day of the 8th month of the lunar month. The date is adjusted every year according to the lunar calendar.

- 3 October – National Foundation Day (개천절 or Gaecheonjeol)

- 9 October – Hangeul Day (한글날 or Hangeulnal)

Pro Tip: Remember, if a public holiday falls on a Sunday, you will get a day off from work on the following Monday.

Planning Your Move to Korea

There are many factors to consider when you are considering relocating you and/or your family to Korea. While the country has come a long way, it still has a bit of a reputation for not welcoming outsiders. Even though some adoptees may identify as being Korean, adoptees are still considered foreigners.

For some Korean adoptees, this can trigger all sorts of complex emotions. Each of us is different, and you should be prepared for what you may experience and embrace whatever feelings may come up for you. There is no right or wrong way to feel. This is your journey; you can choose how you live it.

As you plan to move, you will want to think about your life now in your adoptive country and the things you need to prepare when moving to another country halfway across the world. Not just any country, but your birth place.

It is recommended to create a comprehensive checklist with an estimated date to do some of the following tasks. While completing this ask yourself some of these questions to help you decide how much to move, when to move, and what to move.

Questions to ask yourself:

- How long do I want to stay?
- Do I need to know the language?
- How do I get a job?
- When do I want to go?
- Do I sell my house?
- Do I take my car?
- Do I take my pet?
- Do I take my family?
- Do I cancel my health insurance?
- Where do I store my belongings here while I am gone?

Checklist to do before moving to Korea:

☐ Research or secure a job

☐ Give two-week notice or ask for a leave of absence

☐ Raise enough money for 3-4 months of living expenses

☐ Transfer your money

☐ Exchange your money into KWR

☐ Contact your credit card companies

☐ Contact your banks and consider which accounts to keep open

☐ Cancel your utility services

☐ End your apartment lease or sell or rent your house

☐ Cancel home insurance

☐ Cancel auto insurance

☐ Sell or store your car

☐ Cancel cell phone, cable, and land line services

☐ Stock up on any needed medications

☐ Contact your doctors

☐ Bring your prescriptions

☐ Take some Korean language classes

☐ Store your belongings

☐ Make a list of what to bring

Preparing to Travel

 ## Contact Your Credit Card Company

Contact your credit card company to let them know you will be moving internationally: this will help you avoid any unnecessary holds or potential declines to your credit card. It is recommended you do this for either a traditional credit card or a bank-issued debit card. Most credit card companies and banks allow you to file your travel notification online. You can always call customer service with any questions.

Korean won (KRW). Courtesy of Tara Tenhoff

Cost, Currency, and Conversion

Korea has four types of coins:

₩500 KRW ≈ 45¢ , ₩100 KRW ≈ 9¢, ₩50 KRW ≈ 4¢, and ₩10 KRW ≈ 1¢

Complete set of South Korean coins, photography by Antonia Giordano

25

Bills are ₩1,000 KRW ≈ $1 USD; ₩5,000 KRW ≈ $4.50 USD; ₩10,000 KRW ≈ $9 USD; and ₩50,000 KRW ≈ $45 USD

천원
₩1,000 KRW

오천원
₩5,000 KRW

만원
₩10,000 KRW

오만원
₩50,000 KRW

www.koreaetour.com/interesting-facts-about-korean-money

Don't let all the zeros intimidate you! Most stores accept credit cards, with the exception of the traditional markets.

Exchange Currency with Won

Exchange your currency for Korean "won" (KRW).

- **Local Banks (in the United States)**: You may need to order the won in advance, as some banks do not have foreign currency on hand and may need to order your requested amount of cash. At most banks in the U.S., you can either order the currency at the bank through a teller, or make a request online and it can be mailed to you directly.

- **Incheon Airport**: There are several banks within Incheon Airport where you can exchange foreign currency. Keep in mind that the exchange rate at Incheon is typically the lowest value for your dollar. It is, however, convenient for many travelers.

- **Korean Banks**: KEB Hana Bank, Shinhan Bank, and Woori Bank will allow you to convert your currency for KRW and are prepared to cater to visitors from other countries.

- **Money Changing Stations**: These are forex (foreign exchange) outlets of the aforementioned banks. They can be found predominately in Myeongdong, Dongdaemun, and Itaewon.

Packing for Korea

When you start packing for your move to Korea, it is recommended to create a detailed itemized list to have a record of what is in each box, as well as numbering each box you ship. It would be a good idea to have this list with you just in case your belongings get lost. This document can be in English and does not need to be translated into Korean.

Pro Tip: Whenever you claim your expensive or valuable items such as a computer, television, electronics, or clothing make sure you present your passport at the time.

It is recommended to do your research with the Korean Customs website https://www.customs.go.kr or check with your nearest Korean embassy to make sure you can bring certain belongings to Korea.

Household Items

Common Items that are Prohibited and Restricted

- Foreign currency more than USD $10,000.00
- Recreational narcotics and drugs
- Weapons, firearms, explosives, and ammunition
- Fruit, hay, and seeds
- Plant and plant products
- Beef and pork (must declare to a customs agent)
- Items considered obscene or harmful to national security and the Korean public such as certain printed materials, videos, CDs, etc.

Shipping Your Belongings

Korea is not strict when shipping items. It accepts most household goods if they have been used and are for personal use. But if you bought something specific for Korea, make sure you remove all tags.

You have two options to send your belongings; you can send items by air, which will be the most expensive and most convenient as your items can arrive the same day you arrive in Korea. Another way to send your items is through cargo ship; this way is cheaper, but it will take several months for your items to arrive. Remember, if you ship your items by cargo ship, you need to make sure your items arrive within six months of your arrival to avoid paying duty tax.

Pro Tip: Do not go to the docking port to pick up items you shipped. You will receive a notification when your belongings are ready to be picked up.

Car or Vehicle

If you want to bring a car over, you will need to prove that you will be living in Korea for at least a year or more. You can prove this by providing a one-year contract with a Korean-based employer. If you do not have a contract at this time, you can provide proof of a family member who already resides in Korea.

Before shipping your car, it must be small to midsize. Your car cannot seat more than 10 people. Your car must be owned by you for at least three (3) months or more. Your car will be considered a household item when you ship it.

When shipping your car or motorcycle, you will be exempt from paying duty tax. When your car arrives, you must provide the following documentation to prove it is your car:

- Your employee contract or name and address of a family member who resides in Korea
- Your original certificate/title of ownership/registration
- Your car insurance
- Proof of purchase or loan
- Completed customs declaration form

Pro Tip: If you plan to ship a car, make sure it is not a Japanese make and model, as they are not allowed in Korea. This is the law.

Moving a Pet

You can bring your furry friend with you, but the are some guidelines you will need to follow.

Robin, courtesy of Ami Nafzger

If your pet is from a country that is considered "rabies-free" then there is no mandatory quarantine for your pet. This does not apply if your pet has a current rabies shot. If your pet is from a country where rabies is more prevalent, then your pet will need a blood test and it will need to quarantine.

You will need to show a certificate of proof from a certified veterinarian of your pet's rabies shot given within the last year. If you are bringing a new puppy or kitty, they will need to be vaccinated at six (6) months of age. Also make sure to request your pet have a microchip implanted which can be administered before a rabies vaccination.

Your pet will need to be micro-chipped with an ISO 11784/11785 pet microchip number. This number must be 15 digits and be non-encrypted. If the microchip is not ISO 11784/11785 compliant, you must bring your own microchip scanner. If your scanner does not work when your pet arrives in Korea, your pet may have to be quarantined and you will start the whole process over again.

You will also need to provide a health certificate stating your animal's overall wellbeing. This can only be completed by a certified veterinarian.

Korean customs will accept the following documents as certified health certificates:

- **United States:** Veterinary Health Certificate for Export of Dogs and Cats from the United States of America to Korea
- **Canada:** CFIA International Health Certificate
- **EU:** European Union Pet Passport
- **Australia:** DAFF Export Permit/Health Certificate

Packing for Yourself

Keep an open mind, and understand that the Korean culture will be different than Western cultures. We encourage you to study important words/phrases, learn how to read Korean, and learn how to count in Korean to help you get around easier. Bring a journal which will help you process your journey while starting a new chapter in your life. These are some considerations to help understand yourself while living in the Korean culture.

Bring the following documents:

- Any/all adoption paperwork, and two copies of your passport and possible birth certificate
- An updated resume and duplicate passport-sized photos of yourself
- A copy of your license, diploma, or professional certificates
- An up-to-date passport
- Your driver's license
- A copy of your medical history
- A copy of your COVID-19 vaccination card

Pro Tip: Make sure you scan all these documents and have them downloaded to your computer, tablet, or cell phone, etc.

Bed Linens

In Korea, bed sheets are not common and often hard to find. It is customary to sleep only with comforters, blankets, and pillows.

Deodorant

Since Koreans scientifically do not emit body odor, deodorant is scarce in local stores. Bring at least a few deodorants if you normally use any.

Laptop

Bring your own laptop and electronics from home and be mindful that the plugs will be different internationally.

Power Strips and Plugs

Be sure to bring the appropriate outlet adapter as Korea uses power plugs and socket which are type C and F. The standard voltage is 220 V and the standard frequency is 60 Hz.

Medication

You can find over-the-counter medicine in Korea such as pain and cold medication. With prescription medications, it is recommended to bring your medication(s), rather than trying to find it Korea. If you have a preference of multi-vitamins, then also remember to pack them. Make sure to read the regulations on prescription medications in Korea. Some regulations may be different in Korea than in your hometown and could be considered an illegal substance.

Towels

Koreans use small towels the size of a hand towels that they use to dry themselves off after a shower. If you prefer bigger towels then you can purchase them at large markets such as Costco or H-Mart.

Shower Caddy Organizer

This will help to organize your bathroom items since there is no separation between the shower, toilet, and sink. This way, everything can stay dry and out of the way while you shower. This can also be found at large markets, the same place you buy towels.

Toiletries

You can buy toiletries in Korea such shampoo, soap, Q-tips, toothpaste, feminine products, etc. If you have certain preferences, you may want to consider bringing your own as it may be difficult to find and more expensive.

Clothes

Bring enough clothes if you are bigger and taller. Many Koreans usually have a smaller frame than the body types in Western cultures. Remember, you will be walking a lot in Korea; you will want to bring a comfortable pair of shoes that you can slip on and off. Brand name shoes are more expensive. Hiking is very popular in Korea, so consider bringing or purchasing hiking gear. Bring appropriate clothing for each of the four seasons *(see the Climate section on page 16)*.

Conservative Clothing

Keep in mind that it is customary to dress conservatively in Korea. Some Koreans may expect you to cover up your skin. Korea is changing bit by bit with what they wear, especially the younger generations, but in general, be aware of specific situations and how your dress may affect others. Many people will have their chest and shoulders covered. If you are going to the beach, bring a swim shirt and swim shorts.

Korean Phrase Book or App on Your Phone

If you do not know the Korean language, a Korean phrase book or an app will help you get around. You can refer to the Adoptee Hub guide *Visiting Korea* for more information about the Korean language and culture.

Kybo Bookstore, Seoul, South Korea, photography by Antonia Giordano

Savings

If you can, plan to bring about three to four months of savings for the beginning part of your stay. Even if you have a job already in Korea, you will not get your first paycheck until a month later. Employees in Korea get paid monthly. Also, the savings you bring could be used for an apartment when you first move in.

English Books or Native Language Books

Bring a tablet reader such as a Kindle or an iPad to Korea so you have access to multiple books. Paperback and hard cover books can be found in Seoul at the Kyobo Mungo book store (교보문고).

Vaccination and Health Requirements

Korea requires that all people entering must have their COVID-19 shots, so you will need to provide proof of vaccination. If you have respiratory problems such as asthma, you will want to wear a face mask as the air pollution in Korea could affect you more in the spring and summer. Following is a list of vaccinations that the CDC recommends for you to get before moving to Korea.

Required and recommended vaccines are:

- Measles, mumps, rubella
- COVID-19 and the booster shot
- Flu shot
- Tetanus, diphtheria, and pertussis
- Chickenpox
- Shingles
- Pneumococcal
- Meningitis
- Polio

Employment

Chances are that if you are planning a move to Korea, you might have already found a job, but if you or a family member need to find work this chapter will provide some useful tips. First, it is important to understand requirements and employment in Korea.

Job Requirements

Korea has some standard and strict requirements to be employed in Korea.

1. To be eligible to work in Korea for any job, you need at least an undergraduate university degree.
2. It is preferred if your degree is in the same field as the job you are applying for.
3. Knowledge of the Korean language is not necessarily mandatory, but it is highly advisable.

Understanding Employment

Korea has a growing economy, and the current job market is favorable to foreign workers. If you are worried about having to speak the language, it is still possible to find jobs in Korea that do not require this; however, employers will be more favorable to applicants who know Korean or are interested in learning. Also, this will be an advantage to you in an in-person interview. Your willingness to learn Korean will show the employer that you are committed and interested in living and working in Korea. This will also help you integrate with your coworkers and work culture more fully.

Teaching English is a very popular job for English-speaking job seekers. Teaching English does not require extensive knowledge of Korean and some schools even prefer for teachers to not be bilingual because they want their Korean students to be forced to learn and practice the English language. English proficiency is highly valued in Korea, making English teachers one of the more sought out professions.

If teaching English is not right for you, there are other fields to consider such as information technology, general office administration, manufacturing, and careers related to health, science, research, and technology.

Otherwise working as a self-employed person is more readily accepted in Korea. Working days are the standard Monday through Friday but being self-employed you should be aware that hours can legally be anywhere from 40 to 70 hours per week.

Tips for Getting a Job

In Korea, if you are applying for a job in the corporate field or with some type of learning academy, then hiring can be done differently. Be prepared to provide a professional picture of yourself with a detailed resume of your experience. Many places like to see a picture of you before they consider interviewing you. Koreans are impressed with how you look, dress, and if you have an education, hold degrees, or practice a profession such as lawyer, doctor, Ph.D. scholar, etc.

If you are called in for an in-person interview or online, they may ask you personal questions. Some of the questions may be offensive in Western cultures; however, in Korean culture they are acceptable. For instance, they may ask how old you are? How much money do you make now? What do your parents and/or family do? Why do you want to come live in Korea? Why do you want to work with them? If you are a female, they may even ask you to wear a dress or skirt. They may ask you to work under their visa terms. These are things to be aware of.

Your Résumé

Korea has a specific résumé style that you should follow when applying for a job in Korea. You should download a standard Korean résumé template and fill it in with the relevant information. A sample template is available from our website:
https://adopteehub.org/Korean%20Resume%20Template.docx

Pro Tip: When Korean Human Resources teams go through a large stack of résumés, having a non-Korean style résumé is more likely to hurt your chances rather than help you.

이력서

Passport Photo	성명	한글	Korean Name	지원분야	부서	Department
		영어	English Name		직책	Job Title
	생년월일	DOB		연락처	휴대폰	Mobile Number
	현주소	Address			e-mail	
	취미	Hobby		특기	Special Comment	

학력사항	입학년월일	졸업년월일	학교명	전공	학점
	Enrolment Date	Graduation Date	University	Major	Grade Average

근무기간	근무처	직위	담당업무	퇴직사유

Example of Korean résumé template

Your Personal Information

The first page of a Korean-style résumé will contain personal information such as your address, date of birth, cell phone number, and e-mail. You will also see sections to write any hobbies or special activities you participate in. These are the areas where you can personalize your resume and let your personality and interests show.

Education History

When filling out information about your education history, keep in mind that the Korean grading system may be different from your adoptive country. Use your best estimation to convert your GPA to the Korean equivalent.

Work History

The area, in a standard Korean résumé, designated for your work history is small. This is because Korean employers only expect to see a brief job description such as "I was a Human Resources Specialist" or "I was a Software Developer."

References

One thing you may notice that is missing from a Korean resume is a section for references. This is not a requirement. Instead, Korean employers will contact a previous employer of their choosing without letting you know who they contact. Make sure you inform your past and current employers that you list on your résumé that someone may contact them.

Cover Letter Tips

A cover letter in Korea is also called a "self-introduction" letter (jagiseogaeseo / 자기소개서). As with any cover letter, Korean employers will want to know more specific details about your work history and qualifications that make you the perfect candidate for the position for which you are applying.

Pro Tip: As an applicant, you want to talk about your career growth, your education, your personality, and why you want the job you are applying for.

Interview Tips

When going in for an interview in Korea, you should arrive 10-15 minutes early. Bring printed color copies of your résumé and cover letter, and, if possible, have them in both English and Korean.

Pro Tip: It is traditional in Korea to bow instead of shaking hands when meeting someone. Do not try to shake the interviewer's hand unless they initiate shaking your hand first.

Be aware that the entire interview process could take a few weeks or even a few months. You may also be asked to submit a Test of Proficiency in Korean (TOPIK / 한국어능력시험) score.

Job Searching

Online Job Search

If you are unable to move to Korea before finding a job, here are some online sites in English that would be helpful to you.

* JobKorea.com
* Saramin.com
* PeopleNJob.com
* LinkedIn

Newspapers Job Search

Korean jobs are published in Korean English newspapers. Job postings can be found through online newspapers or printed newspapers in Korea. Three big newspapers to check out are:

* The Korea Herald
* The Korea Times
* The Seoul Times

Job Fair

Korea hosts annual job fairs that specifically target foreigners. These job fairs will typically be split into two different categories:

* Job fairs for international students
* Job fairs for international residents

To find the date of these fairs, you can search online for the following terms:

* Job fair for international students
  (Oeguginyuhaksaeng chaeyongbangnamhoe / 외국인유학생 채용박람회)
* Job fair for foreign residents
  (Oegugin chwieopbangnamhoe / 외국인 취업박람회)

Although these job fairs are for foreigners, it is best to come with printed copies of your résumé, a cover letter written in both English and Korean, and a picture of yourself.

Networking Tips

As an overseas adoptee, you may find yourself warmly welcomed in Korea. This will be helpful when it comes to networking as you will find many Korean nationals will be happy to speak with you.

Receiving a business card from an employer is considered an invitation to contact them, in Korea. If you receive a business card from someone, be sure to follow up with an e-mail afterward.

> **Pro Tip: You should have business cards made in English and Korean and make sure to always carry them with you.**

In addition to networking with Korean nationals, it is also a good idea to network with other foreigners as they will be the most familiar with what it's like working in Korea.

> **Pro Tip: It is recommended to apply for the F-4 visa (which was established in Korea for Korean adoptees and overseas Koreans in 1999). This way you are free to leave an employer and work for another company without having to leave the country and renew your visa. (See Chapter 17 regarding how to register for an F-4 visa.)**

Average Salary in Korea

For people who teach English in Korea, there is a reputation that you could earn a lot of money. This is because many foreign English teachers have opportunities to be offered free accommodations and health insurance. The average salary for a foreign English teacher in Korea is about ₩45 million KRW ($38,000 USD) a year. But if you work in Seoul it is ₩65 million KRW ($55,500 USD).

Pro Tip: In Korea, you will get paid monthly, not weekly or biweekly. Make sure you have enough funds to support yourself and or your family until you get paid. Many companies will automatically deposit your salary in your bank account; however, some employers will provide you with a large envelope with your monthly salary. Be mindful of where you travel after receiving this cash.

Below is a chart of monthly salaries for professional jobs in Korea:

Job	KRW per Mo.	USD per Mo.
Editor/Content Writer	₩2,000,000 - 5,500,000	$1,680 - 4,600
Sales and Marketing	₩1,500,000 - 4,200,000	$1,260 - 3,540
Public Relations	₩2,000,000 - 5,000,000	$1,680 - 4,200
Securities Analyst	₩3,000,000 - 7,700,000	$2,530 - 6,500
Programmers and Developers	₩1,500,000 - 4,200,000	$1,260 - 3,540
Project Manager	₩4,000,000 - 5,600,000	$3,370 - 4,700
Teacher (English)	₩1,860,000 - 3,000,000	$1,570 - 2,530
Software Engineer	₩78,454,200+	$6,040+

Other Jobs	KRW Annual	USD Annual
Architect	₩37,716,000	$31,680
Marketing Manager	₩63,131,000	$53,030
Product Manager	₩72,400,400	$60,940
Web Developer	₩51,425,700	$43,200
UX Designer	₩55,300,000	$46,450
Teacher	₩54,302,200	$45,700
Accountant	₩55,104,000	$46,290
Nurse	₩41,257,600	$34,700

Chart of average monthly salaries, Internations.org 1

Self-Employment

In Korea, self-employment is common. You will find plenty of competition, so to go this route you will need to arrive with an impressive portfolio, client base, references, and sample projects demonstrating your best work. You will also have the added benefit of setting your schedule and pay. Popular platforms in Korea to find freelance work include:

- https://www.fiverr.com
- https://www.upwork.com
- https://www.wishket.com
- https://soomgo.com

[1] Your Guide on Jobs and Finding Work in South Korea. InterNations. (n.d.). Retrieved January 30, 2022, from https://www.internations.org/go/moving-to-south-korea/working

Office Buildings, Seoul, South Korea, photography by Antonia Giordano

Business Culture

If you are going to be working in a Korean company office there are certain business cultural practices you should be aware of as Korean society is deeply rooted in their long-standing traditions of respect and hierarchy.

When greeting someone for the first time, you should wait to be introduced by a third party. Remember it is more customary to bow than shake hands. You should greet someone by their formal title and use your title as well. This will immediately establish hierarchy. If you don't know their title, you will want to ask.

Business Cards

Exchanging business cards when first meeting someone is common. The giving and receiving of a business card should be done with both hands. As a business card is seen as the extension of a person in Korea, it should be treated with the utmost respect. Do not simply slide it into your pocket. Instead, place it on the table in front of you for the duration of the meeting and then put it in a specific business cardholder.

Pro Tip: Read the card and show interest in who you are meeting and talking to at that time.

Hierarchy

As mentioned above, it is important to establish hierarchy right away because this is an important part of Korean work culture. Korea has great respect for seniority, both in age and profession. Business decisions are typically made as a group but start in order of hierarchy.

Should you meet a business associate who "outranks" you, then you should show them a good deal of respect. If you are senior to someone, you should still treat them with respect and humility, as these are important traits in Korean society.

Do not be surprised if someone you are senior to does not make much eye contact during a meeting. This tendency is changing in more modern Korean society, but some of your colleagues may still follow these traditions.

> **Pro Tip: Be aware of the direct eye contact you make with someone senior to you. It is considered not polite to make eye contact with your senior.**

Gift Giving

In the U.S. it is not expected to give gifts to your boss or seniors; however, gift-giving is common in Korea and it is important to bring one when you first meet a business partner. Just like with the business cards, the gift should be presented with both hands. If you are giving a gift to more than one person, the gift with the greatest value should go to the most senior person you meet or will be working with.

Meetings

In Korean business culture, a meeting is usually scheduled a few weeks in advance and do not be surprised if the meeting is canceled at the last minute. This is not meant to be rude. However, if a meeting is canceled more than once then it may be a sign from your Korean colleagues that they do not want to have the meeting. When scheduling these meetings, they should only be scheduled between 10 AM - 12 PM and 2 PM - 4:00 PM.

Pro Tip: In Korean business, they like to use the military time when scheduling meetings, for example, for 2:00 PM, they would say 14:00 hours.

Punctuality & Dress Code

Punctuality is seen as a sign of respect in Korea. You should always be 10 to 15 minutes early, even if everyone else is late. If you think you will be late, you should inform someone from your team that you still intend to attend the meeting.

Korean culture leans towards conservative clothing, especially in the workplace. Men should wear white button-up shirts with dark suits and women should also wear darker-colored business suits. Most employers prefer women to wear skirt suits.

Starting a Business in Korea

If you are planning on working for yourself or starting your own business in Korea, there are several steps you'll need to follow:

1. Research

Research the company or industry you are interested in. There are expectations rules and regulations you'll need to follow.

2. Naming

Pick a name for your business. Find out on the internet to see what names are out there in Korea and/or around the world. You will need to register your web domain and make sure the name you want for your business does not exist yet. Your business name will need to be written in Korean to register it.

3. Business Plan

Have a business plan that includes a clear vision, goals, and objectives that have a description of your business identity and outline sustainability and success.

4. Visa

Apply for an F-4 visa. This way you can live and run your business while being in Korea. Having an F-4 visa can help you to gain more freedom and make it easier to file paperwork for starting a business in Korea.

5. Location

If you are looking for a physical space to rent or purchase, work with a real estate leasing office to secure a place. It's important to obtain the necessary paperwork to register your business. You will also need to provide a large sum of money to rent or purchase the space.

6. Bank Accounts

Open a bank account using the legal name of your business at a Korean bank. To start a bank account, you will need to provide a valid passport and deposit at least ₩4,100,000 KRW in your bank account. Be sure to label this money as "For Investment Purposes Only."

7. Registering

After opening an account in Korea and receiving documentation from a bank, you can then register your business name. Complete this in the following order:

1. Complete a registration form at the nearest government offices to get approval
2. Then make a declaration of the business
3. Then take the documents from the bank and the real estate lease to the local district office to register the name of your business
4. Take care that your business name is written in Korean
5. Wait a few days for the paperwork to process

8. Incorporation

Next, you'll need to choose a business structure and its entity. Look at the incorporation requirements and costs of the business entities as a guide. You will also want to research how taxes work in Korea. There are five structures you can choose from:

- Joint Stock Company
- Limited Liability Company
- Private Limited Company
- General Partnership Company
- Limited Partnership Company
- Open a branch company in Korea. You'll have to get the branch to a specific foreign exchange bank and complete court and business registrations.

9. Notarize

It's important to notarize all your documents so everything can be finalized and the founder can be appointed for registration.

10. Taxes

Identify tax-related laws that may apply to your business. Then apply for a tax registration payment certificate. You'll need to attach copies of this certificate to every transaction you make for your business.

When you file taxes for your business, you will need to provide the following:

- Your passport
- Your F-4 visa
- Your business name registration
- Your bank account documentation is available for the local district office to look at
- Other documents that could be required

11. Insurance

Work with an insurance broker to help you to obtain insurance and address any pension issues. You are required and expected to visit government agencies including the:

- National Pension Fund
- Public Health Insurance Program
- Employment Insurance

12. Marketing

Market your business through word of mouth, visual props, social media, sales, and promotions to get customers in Korea interested in your business. Build your website, network, partner with others, etc.

13. Opening

Welcome your new customers at a soft opening and a grand opening. Your business may be required to get permission to have a soft and a grand opening, you will need to contact the local district office. It is a good idea to get permission before you have an opening.

Getting an Education in Korea

Korea is known to be one of the most educated countries in the world. More than half the population of Korea has some degree of higher education. School standards are so high that even a free public schools might be mistaken for a private school, which can cost equivalent to $13,000-$34,000 USD.

The education system usually requires students to attend 12-16 hours of schooling per day. The school system is test-focused and goal-orientated. For example, on the second Tuesday of November upwards of 600,000 college bound students will take the College Scholastic Aptitude Test (CSAT). This is an eight-hour-long test taken all over the country from 8:00 AM - 5:00 PM. Students are tested on their knowledge of Korean, English, mathematics, Korean history, a second foreign language or Chinese characters, and two additional subjects. They have breaks in-between each part of the test and given time for lunch.

The CSAT is taken very seriously, so much so that on the day of the test businesses open later so that there are no traffic jams and students can get to the test on time. Public transportation even runs more frequently than normal and students that get stuck can be escorted by police. Even air traffic is cleared to guarantee complete silence for all the students to focus.

Children at school; Seoul, Korea; photography by Antonia Giordano

Children attending school as foreigners are expected to speak Korean. Childcare for younger children can cost about $200-$400 USD a month.

Below are some common cultural practices in Korean schools and the education system:

- Assignments and study time are assigned individually. It is rare for students to work in groups or have discussions.

- Uniforms are mandatory in all middle and high schools.

- Students stay in the same room throughout the day while teachers change from classroom to classroom.

- Students spend most of their days at school; not surprisingly, classrooms are treated like homes. Students clean their space either before or after classes. There is also a strict no-shoe policy, and most children wear slippers or inside shoes.

- Skipping school is extremely rare in Korea. Students that want to show their rebellious side tend to just use their smart-phones during class.

- Attending school every other Saturday was mandatory in some schools up until 2012. These days, public schools are not allowed to hold classes on weekends. However, some other institutions such as private schools and academies still have weekend classes.

University

Getting a university degree is a must in Korea, otherwise, a person is considered a second-class citizen. University tuition fees in Korea will range between $2,100 to $6,500 USD per year.

As an international student at a university, especially if you are interested in science, technology, or engineering, you will find excellent programs at Korean universities. Korea's educational system emphasizes research and innovation. If you are interested in being at the forefront of technological advances or scientific discoveries, then you should find comfort in the Korea education system. Some Korean universities, such as KAIST (listed below) place special emphasis on robotic technology and research that will ultimately improve societies around the globe.

Also, if you want to become a teacher, teachers are highly regarded in Korea and are often admired as authority figures. Therefore, studying to become a teacher is one of the most desirable professions in the country. Because of this popularity, getting a teacher's license can also be challenging. Those who do obtain a license to practice can expect to get a high-paying job.

Children at school; Seoul, Korea; photography by Antonia Giordano

Requirements

In addition to maintaining an excellent grade point average (GPA) and academic record, studying at a Korean university will also generally require the following from you as a student:

- Ability to attain a visa (i.e. no criminal record)
- Proficiency in English as many university courses are taught in this language
- IELTS scores (if coming from a non-English speaking country)
- Basic knowledge of Korean
- Valid passport and immunization records

When to Apply

Korean universities run on a two-semester academic calendar. The academic year typically starts in March, but some universities will allow students to enter either semester. Prospective students interested in spring enrollment must submit their application in the fall of the previous year, and students wanting to start in the fall must submit their application in the summer of the same year in which they hope to start attending classes.

Korean universities follow a fall and spring semester schedule like the United States. Primary schools follow a different schedule with the academic year lasting from March to February with breaks from mid-July to the end of August and mid-February to the beginning of March. That's right-- Korean students go to school during the summertime and all year long with small breaks.

The Best Universities for International Students in Korea

Competition to get into Korean universities is stiff. If you want to enroll in a Korean university, you should be sure you have an outstanding profile.

The application will be competitive, but do not let that dissuade you. Korea is extremely open to foreigners, especially international students. Many Korean universities even offer generous scholarships just for international students.

In no particular order, here are some top universities for international students:

- Seoul National University (서울대학교)
- Korea Advanced Institute for Science and Technology (한국과학기술원) (KAIST)
- Pohang University of Science and Technology (포항공과대학교) (POSTECH)
- Korea University
- Sungkyunkwan University (성균관대학교)
- Yonsei University (연세대학교)

F-4 Visa

The F-4 visa was created and came into law in 1999. Before this visa, Korean adoptees had to leave Korea every three months and renew their visas. Adoptees had no basic rights in Korea and were treated like foreigners. They couldn't even buy cell phones and always needed a Korean national to sponsor them. Many adoptees went to Japan and would stay overnight until the paperwork for their visa was renewed.

Over time, this became costly and very inconvenient for people of Korean ancestry who had returned and were trying to reside in Korea. In 1997, Ami Nafzger, founder and first Secretary-General of G.O.A'L (Global Overseas Adoptees Link), worked tirelessly alongside the Korean government and petitioned to create a special visa for all overseas Korean adoptees worldwide; at the time this was some 200,000 plus people. Because of these efforts, G.O.A'L was approved for securing a special visa for all adoptees and all overseas Koreans worldwide. This is now called the F-4 visa. Today, thousands of Korean adoptees, overseas Korean immigrants and their children, and their children's children, from all around the world, can return to Korea indefinitely and reside there under the F-4 visa.

The F-4 visa is a visa that is granted to those of Korean descent. It is a renewable permanent resident visa that is valid for 2–3 years. After it expires, one does not need to leave the country to renew it, you can stay in Korea to renew it there. It allows you to enjoy most of the benefits Korean nationals have.

Summary of the Application Process

1. Make sure you double-check all the required documents described below.

   - A passport must be valid for 3 plus years remaining
   - One to two color copies of your passport
   - Two current passport photos 3.5 x 4.5 cm, must be no older than 6 months
   - Completed Adoption Certificate 입양 사실확인서

- Korean Family Registry:
  - Family Relation Certificate 가족관계증명서
  - Identification Certificate 기본증명서
  - -or- Removal from Registry Certificate 제적등본
- Certificate of Citizenship/Naturalization 외국국적 취득 관련 서류
- Immigration fee, ₩130,000 KRW cash only
- Lease/Rental contract & confirmation applications 고소 신고 (신청)서 and 고소 신고 (신청)
- Completed application form 통합신청서
- Apostilled criminal background check from adoptive country

2. Register for an appointment
   a. Register for an appointment at https://ww.kikorea.go.kr
   b. You will need your passport number to make an appointment
3. When you arrive for your appointment
   a. Make sure you arrive 10-15 minutes early
   b. Wait for your number to be called
   c. Provide your application and required documents to the immigration officer
   d. If your application is approved, you will be directed to the payment area to pay your fees
   e. After you pay your fees, you should go back to the immigration officer and show your receipt to confirm that you paid
   f. When the immigration officer confirms your application and payment, the immigration officer will give an application receipt to confirm your number
   g. You will need to ask when you can pick up your Alien Registration Card (ARC) if they do not tell you otherwise
4. Wait 2-4 weeks
   a. It will take 2-4 weeks to process your F-4 visa
   b. Immigration will give you a date when you can pick up your ARC, at this time, you can ask them to send it to you via mail
   c. You can check your application status by calling 1345

Pro Tip: If you leave Korea during the time immigration is processing your F-4 visa application, your application will be canceled and not processed. Stay in the country until you receive your visa.

5. Pick up your ARC
    a. On the designated date go back to the immigration office where you applied and pick up your ARC.
    b. If you choose to have this card mailed to you, it will arrive within 4 weeks. This will cost about ₩3,000 KRW.
6. Take note of your responsibilities after you obtain an F-4 visa and ensure to follow the F-4 visa rules. If you do not, this may affect your future visa renewals. You must:
    a. Update your address whenever it changes
    b. Update any changes in your passport number
    c. Report any changes to your personal information
    d. File for Korean taxes
    e. Apply to renew your F-4 visa 60 days before it expires
    f. Notify immigration if you plan to leave Korea for an extended period.

Pro Tip: If you apply for the F-4 visa abroad (outside of Korea) the fees may vary.

7. The total amount of application fees is ₩130,000 KRW ($130.00 USD)
    a. Korean cash only
    b. The application fee is about ₩100,000 KRW
    c. Alien Registration Card (ARC) fee is about ₩30,000 KRW
    d. Family Registry Fee is about ₩1,000 KRW

A Step-by-Step Guide for the F-4 Visa

This information is subject to change and only reflect policies as of 2021.

사증발급신청서
VISA APPLICATION FORM

<신청서 작성방법>
▶ 신청인은 사실에 근거하여 빠짐없이 정확하게 신청서를 작성해야 합니다.
▶ 신청서상의 모든 질문에 대한 답변은 한글 또는 영문으로 기재해야 합니다.
▶ 선택사항은 해당 칸[　] 안에 √ 표시를 하시기 바랍니다.
▶ '기타' 를 선택한 경우, 상세내용을 기재하시기 바랍니다.
<How to fill out this form>
▶ The applicant must fill out this form completely and correctly.
▶ The applicant must write in block letters either in English or Korean.
▶ For multiple-choice questions, the applicant must check [√] all that apply.
▶ If the applicant selects 'Other' , please provide more information in the given space.

---

1. 인적사항 / PERSONAL DETAILS

PHOTO 여권용 사진 (35㎜×45㎜) - 흰색 바탕에 모자를 쓰지 않은 정면 사진으로 촬영일 부터 6개월이 경과하지 않아 야 함 A color photo taken within the last 6 months (full face without hat, front view against white or off-white background)	1.1 여권에 기재된 영문 성명/Full name in English (as shown in passport)

1.1 여권에 기재된 영문 성명/Full name in English (as shown in passport)

성 Family Name	명 Given Names

1.2 한자성명 漢字姓名	1.3 성별 Sex 남성/Male[　] 여성/Female[　]
1.4 생년월일 Date of Birth (yyyy/mm/dd)	1.5 국적 Nationality
1.6 출생국가 Country of Birth	1.7 국가신분증번호 National Identity No.

1.8 이전에 한국에 출입국하였을 때 다른 성명을 사용했는지 여부

　Has the applicant ever used any other names to enter or depart Korea?

　아니요 No [　]　예 Yes [　]　→ '예' 선택 시 상세내용 기재 If 'Yes' , please provide details

　(성 Family Name　　　　　　　　　　, 명 Given Name　　　　　　　　　　　)

1.9 복수 국적 여부 Is the applicant a citizen of more than one country ?　아니요 No [　]　예 Yes [　]

　→ '예' 선택 시 상세내용 기재 If 'Yes' , please write the countries (　　　　　　　　　　　　)

---

2. 신청 사증 정보/ DETAILS OF VISA APPLICATION

2.1 체류기간(장·단기) Period of Stay(Long/Short-term) 90일 이상 장기체류 Long-term Stay over 90 days 　[　] 90일 이하 단기체류 Short-term Stay less than 90 days 　[　]	2.2 체류자격 Status of Stay

---

공용란 FOR OFFICIAL USE ONLY

기본사항	체류자격	체류기간	사증종류	단수·복수(2회, 3회 이상)
접수사항	접수일자	접수번호	처리과	
허가사항	허가일자	사증번호	고지사항	
결 재	담당자	<심사의견> 가 [　] 부 [　]		

< 수입인지 부착란 >

F-4 Visa Application Form

How to Apply

1. Visit https://goal.or.kr/f-4-visa

2. You are encouraged to signup and become a member of G.O.A'L in order to obtain proper paperwork

3. Review application form (통합신청서)

4. Provide a valid passport and color copy. Your passport must be valid for three or more years at the time of application

5. Provide two current passport photos

    a. Both photos must be 3.5 x 4.5 cm

    b. Both photos must be identical

    c. Both photos must be less than 6 months old at the time of the application

    d. You can order these in your adoptive country or Korea

6. Obtain an adoption certificate (입양 사실확인서). You must request your adoption certificate through your adoption agency located in Korea. Read your adoption paperwork carefully to find one of these agency's name listed on the next page. This will include your:

    a. Korean name

    b. English name (legal adoptive name) must match your passport

    c. Korean ID #

Pro Tip: Information requested may vary between your U.S. adoption agency and your Korean adoption agency. Please refer to your paperwork from your Korean agency. Contact the agency with any questions or issues.

    d. Legal residence in Korea

    e. Name(s) of adoptive parent(s)

    f. Country of adoption

    g. Date of adoption

    h. Reason for issuance

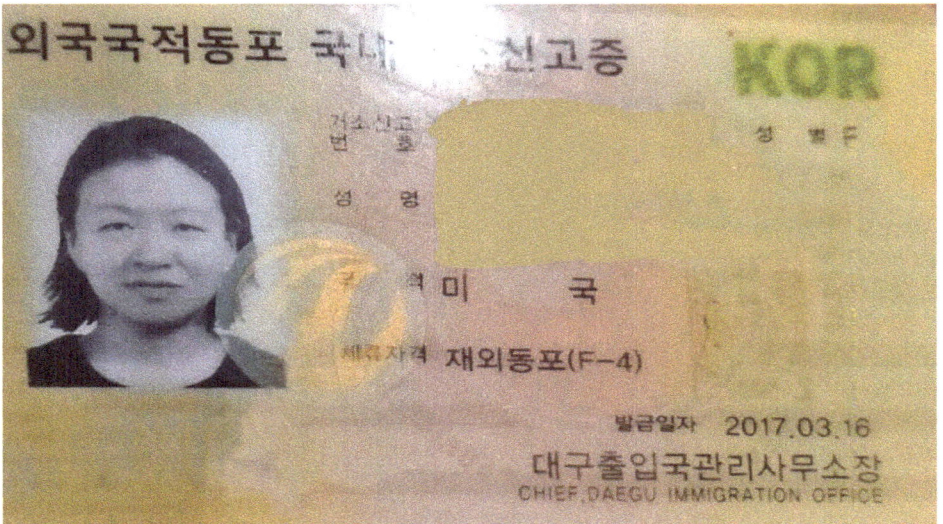

Example adoptee F4 Visa card, photography by Antonia Giordano

Pro Tip: Once you receive your adoption certificate from your Korean adoption agency, it is only valid for three months from the date received.

You will provide this information to your Korean adoption agency:

- Legal name (exact spelling on your passport)
- Korean name (before your adoption)
- Date of adoption (if known)
- Adoptive father's first and last name
- Country of adoption
- Scanned copy of your passport

Pro Tip: Documents must be original and no older than six months

Adoption agency contact information in Korea:

Eastern Social Welfare Society (ESWS)

Email: postadoption@eastern.or.kr
Phone: 02-332-3941 (in Korea)
Phone: +82-2-332-3941 (from overseas)

Eastern Social Welfare Society; Seoul, Korea; photography by Antonia Giordano

Korean Social Services (KSS)

Email: kssinc@kssinc.org
Phone: 02-908-9191 (in Korea)
Phone: +82-2-908-9191 (from overseas)

Korean Social Services; Seoul, Korea; courtesy of Ami Nafzger

Holt Korea

Email: holtkorea@hotmail.com
Phone: 02-6938-5550 (in Korea)
Phone: +82-2-6938-5550 (from overseas)

Holt Korea; Seoul, Korea; photography by Antonia Giordano

Social Welfare Society (SWS)

Email: swspas@sws.or.kr
Phone: 02-567-8891 (in Korea)
Phone: +82-2-567-8891 (from overseas)

Social Welfare Society; Seoul, Korea; courtesy of Ami Nafzger

7. Provide one of the following pertaining to the Korean Family Registry

   a. Family Relation Certificate (가족관계증명서)

   b. Identification Certificate (기본증명서)

   c. -or- Removal from Registry Certificate (제적등본)

Pro Tip: The date your Korean citizenship was rescinded must be on the basic Identification Certificate.

8. Perform the following to obtain your Family Registry

   • Visit any community service center (동사무소 / 주민센터) with your adoption certificate and passport

   • If applying abroad, you need to sign a power of attorney, allowing your nearest Korean embassy/Korean consulate to request these documents from Korea on behalf of you

Pro Tip: There is a small fee, about $1.00 USD per document.

Pro Tip: G.O.A'L is the official translation center for adoptees. This is authorized by the Korean Ministry of Justice-Immigration Service Department.

9. Provide your Certificate of Citizenship/Naturalization (외국국적 취득 관련 서류)

   a. Issued by your adoptive country as proof of citizenship

   b. Prepare 1-2 color copies

   c. This document should be translated into Korean

Pro Tip: If you are a U.S. citizen, you are required to present your original certificate for inspection. A U.S. passport is not proof of citizenship.

10. Provide a lease or rental contract (고소 신고 (신청)서); a lease assumes some ownership.

Leasing:

    a. You will need proof of residence which can be a copy of your housing contract or a lease agreement

    b. Complete the application form (고소 신고 (신청)서)

    c. Provide a copy of the landlord's /tenant's ID Card

    d. Provide a certified copy of the deed agreement

    e. Provide a Confirmation of Residence Form (거주 / 숙소제공 확인서)

Renting:

    a. You will need confirmation of your residence

    b. Complete the accommodation report form, a.k.a. the Residence Report form (application form) (고소 신고 (신청)서), shown below.

    c. Provide a copy of the landlord's /tenant's ID Card

    d. Provide a certified copy of the rental agreement

    e. Provide a confirmation of Residence Accommodation Form (거주 / 숙소제공 확인서)

고소 신고 (신청)서

■ 재외동포의 출입국과 법적 지위에 관한 법률 시행규칙 [별지 제1호서식]

거소 신고(신청)서
RESIDENCE REPORT FORM (APPLICATION FORM)

PHOTO
여권용사진
(35mm×45mm)

국내거소신고 및
재발급신청 시에간 부착

Photo required only for issuance/re-issuance of Domestic Residence Card

❶ [　] 외국국적동포 국내거소신고　DOMESTIC RESIDENCE REPORT OF FOREIGN NATIONAL KOREAN

❷ [　] 국내거소 이전신고　REPORT ON ALTERATION OF DOMESTIC RESIDENCE

❸ [　] 국내거소신고증 재발급신청　APPLICATION FOR REISSUANCE OF DOMESTIC RESIDENCE CARD

※ 아래의 작성방법에 따라 기재하고, [　]에는 해당되는 곳에 '√'표를 합니다.
Complete the form as indicated. Tick '√' where applicable.

공통 기재사항 MANDATORY QUESTIONS		
성 Family name	명 Given Name	漢字 姓名
국적 Nationality	생년월일 Date of Birth	성별 Sex　[　]남 M [　]여 F
여권번호 Passport No.	여권발급일 Passport Issue Date	여권유효기간 Passport Expiry Date
국내거소 Residential Address in Korea		전화번호 Phone No.
		휴대전화번호 Cell Phone No.

63

거주/숙소제공 확인서
(Confirmation of Residence/Accommodation)

1. 거주/숙소를 제공 받는 외국인 (Foreign Tenant / Recipient)				
국 적 (Nationality)		외국인등록(거소)번호 (Alien/Domestic Residence Registration No.)		
성 명 (Full Name)			전화번호 (Telephone No.)	
			휴대전화 (Cell phone No.)	
주 소 (Address)				
2. 거주/숙소 제공자 (Landlord / Provider)				
국 적 (Nationality)		주민/외국인등록번호 (Resident/Alien Registration No.)		

6. Include an apostilled criminal background check from adoptive country:

    a. If a citizen of the U.S., you must provide proof of a FBI background check

    b. If a citizen of Europe, you must provide proof of a national police check

    c. If a citizen of Australia, you must provide proof of a national police check

    d. Your criminal background check must be apostilled. An "apostille" is a form of authentication issued to documents for use in countries that participate in the Hague Convention of 1961. An apostille from your adoptive country will authenticate the seals and signatures of officials on public documents such as birth certificates, court orders, or any other document issued by a federal agency that certifies the document(s) so that documentation can be recognized and accepted in foreign countries that are a member of the Hague Apostille Convention. Allow 4-14 days for standard processing from an apostille notary

    e. Visit the following for more information
        https://www.northwestregisteredagent.com/start-a-business/apostille

Pro Tip: Due to COVID-19, the processing time for background checks has increased so plan accordingly.

Non-Korean Descent

If your spouse or partner is of non-Korean descent, they will not qualify for the F-4 visa. However, whatever visa they will be under, they can use it to become a resident in Korea. This will help them to obtain some public benefits.

Social Security and Benefits

A social security number is a 13-digit number that all residents, both national and foreigners, are required to have. This number is known as a resident registration number.

This resident registration number can be referred to in one of two ways:

- Jumin deungnok beonho/주민등록번호
- Deungnok beonho/등록번호

You will need this number to set up a bank account, get a Korean phone number, and do other needed tasks when residing in Korea.

When you apply for a social security number in Korea, depending on where you live, you will need to visit the appropriate immigration office branch for your specific region.

To apply, you will need:

- Completed application
- Passport
- Passport-sized photograph
- Adoption Paperwork Certificate from the adoption agency
- Supporting documents that are related to your visa

Social Security and Health Insurance Benefits

Part of Korea's social security pays into public health insurance. You can take part in public health insurance once you are a registered Korean resident. You will be automatically enrolled after 6 months as a resident in Korea. The current monthly premium is ₩122,880 KRW. Insurance is not provided the first 6 months of employment.

The other part of your social security is paid into the country's national pension plan, which acts as a retirement fund for you and your spouse/partner. If you do not plan on remaining in Korea for more than five years, you may be able to receive the amount you paid as a lump sum upon your departure from Korea.

Taxes

English teachers and foreign engineers are exempt from taxes for the first few years, but other people staying a long time must pay income tax (ranging from 6-45%), a resident's tax (which is 10% of their income tax amount) and are expected to pay into the National Pension Scheme (similar to a 401K).

Depending on nationality, some foreigners can request all their pension payments back at the end of their stay in Korea and can claim some of their taxes back at the end of each tax year.

Dual Citizenship

G.O.A'L petitioned and worked alongside the Korean government to allow adoptees to become Korean citizens without losing their adoption identity, thus securing an option for adoptees to apply for dual citizenship if they are interested.

What to Consider

Getting dual citizenship and walking through this process can be a very emotional process, since we were citizens at one time, but lost this when we were adopted. This is an opportunity for you as an adoptee to have a choice, as an adult, and claim your citizenship back.

There are many things to think about before considering and applying for dual citizenship.

The Benefits of a Dual Citizenship
- You will have access to all Korean websites
- You will have an easier time making financial transactions
- You will have voting rights in Korea, just as a Korean national
- You will receive more Korean government support

Some Disadvantages May Occur
- You may not qualify any longer for a National Institute for International Education (NIIED) - 국립국제교육원 scholarship
- You may have restricted access to diplomatic services in your adoptive country
- You may have a language barrier in Korea while trying to navigate national services
- You may have future travel restrictions overseas to other countries and may not be able to travel outside of Korea as freely
- You may have job limitations due to limited language, knowledge, and cultural differences

- If you have any dependents, your children may have similar disadvantages in their future
- Depending on you and your dependent's age and gender, serving in the Korean military for two years may be mandatory

More Things to Consider

- There is a lengthy application process
- You will need to spend several months in Korea and be unable to travel outside of the country during this time
- You will need to obtain a permanent Korean phone number and address
- You will need to think about if you can speak Korean well enough
- You will need to understand any requirements if you become a Korean citizen for life

Documents You Need to Complete

How to Apply

You will need 4 application forms. Refer to the end of this section for an example of each. This information is subject to change and only reflects policies as of 2021. Visit https://goal.or.kr/dual-citizenship for more information.

1. **Application to Recover Korean Citizenship:** 국적희북혀가 신청서

   This is a three-page document and it will ask you several things you will want to prepare and think about

   - You will need to provide a good contact number and be available to answer questions if they arise. If you choose to leave Korea during the application process, make sure your Korean phone works when you are abroad. You must always be available to be reached by the Korean government during this process

   - You will have to provide your Korean address since your application notification will be sent via MMS

   - You will need the date you lost your citizenship. This is usually the date when you were adopted

   - You will need to explain why you want to change your citizenship

- You will need to outline your education in Korea or your adopted country
- You will need to give details about your career in Korea or your adopted country

Pro Tip: Make sure all your forms are translated to Korean and submitted to the Korean government.

- You will need to provide your capacity to financially sustain, such as your current income and if you are able to sustain your income as a Korean citizen
- Additionally, you will be asked about your family and their residence in Korea; many adoptees will not have this information if they have not found their birth family or reunited with their birth family. You can still apply for dual citizenship, the Korean government will understand that you may not have a family in Korea

2. **Application Form:** Written Statement 진술서

   The Written Statement is a three-page document. You will need to provide:

   - A detailed description of how you think you will obtain foreign citizenship in Korea. For example, it could be through your birth family, marriage, etc.
   - A detailed statement of what kind of life you will have in Korea, your relations, and your career plans after you gain foreign citizenship in Korea
   - A detailed explanation of why you want to recover your Korean citizenship. Include how it would impact your social activities, family, your future, your health, business, your career, your education, etc.
   - A detailed plan about your living plans in Korea, your interests, and your future plans in Korea after you receive your dual citizenship
   - When you had Korean citizenship but lost it through adoption, and why you are attempting to recover your Korean citizenship now
   - If you ever committed treason or any harm to society

- When you were a Korean citizen, did you break any laws? Since we were small children, you would want to reply with N/A (not applicable)
- Did you lose your Korean citizenship due to avoiding your military service in Korea? Since we were small children, you would want to reply with N/A (not applicable)

3. **Application Form:** Personal Statement 신원진술사

The Personal Statement is a two-page document that will ask you for personal/private identifying information on yourself and your immediate family, both birth and adoptive. This includes demographic information and physical characteristics.

4. **Application Form:** Family Relations 가족관계 통보서

This document asks you for personal/private identifying information on your extended family, relatives, and in-laws, both birth and adoptive.

In addition to the 4 documents from above, you will need to submit the following information:

1. Valid passport plus a color copy (refer to the F-4 visa process for more information)
2. Three current passport photos (refer to the F-4 visa process for more information)
3. Certificate of Citizenship/Naturalization (외국국적 취득 관련 서류) Original copy plus one additional copy that is translated into Korean (refer to the F-4 visa process for more information)
4. Adoption Certificate (입양 사실확인서) (refer to the F-4 visa process for more information)
5. Apostilled Criminal Background Check from Adoptive Country (refer to the F-4 visa process for more information)
6. Korean Family Registry or Indivual Registry, if removed from Korean family registry (refer to the F-4 visa process for more information). For Dual Citizenship all 3 documents are required
   - Family Relation Certificate 가족관계증명서
   - Identification Certificate 기본증명서
   - - or- Removal from Registry Certificate 제적등본
7. F-4 visa, (ARC) Alien Registration Card (original card plus one copy of the front and back)

8. **Additional Documents:** It is recommended to contact FOIA for these and follow the application process in the United States if that is your adoptive country. FOIA stands for the Freedom of Information Act. It is a law that requires the full or partial disclosure of previously unreleased information and documents controlled by the United States government upon request.

   a. Name change

   b. Change of birth date (It is recommended to contact FOIA and follow the application process in the United States if your adoptive country is the United States)

   c. All adoption-related documents (It is recommended to contact FOIA and follow the application process in the United States if your adoptive country is the United States)

   d. All adoption-related documents (court decree of adoption, birth certificate, all other related adoption documents.) Documents must be the originals

   e. Marriage certificate

9. You will need to provide ₩200,000 KRW in cash only

Time Line for Approval

Wait for your Application to be Processed

- The processing time will take up to 6 months to 1 year

- Make sure you are available whether overseas or in Korea to answer any questions the Korean government may have

- MMS notification or letter will let you know the application was processed

Attend an Oath Ceremony

- MMS will send you a time and place for the oath ceremony, your attendance is mandatory

- Attend the ceremony, make sure you are dressed up. This is a special occasion

- Follow directions and do as you are requested

Sign the Pledge

- You will need to wait two weeks to sign the pledge of becoming a Korean citizen

- The pledge states that "you will not exercise your foreign rights within the Republic of Korea" now that you officially are a Korean citizen.

- When you sign the pledge, you must bring the following:
    - Your ARC card plus a copy of it (front and back)
    - Your passport plus a copy of it
    - Your Certificate of Citizenship / Naturalization (original needed if a US citizen)
    - Your Family Registry

Pro Tip: During this time, you are not allowed to leave Korea until you obtain your Korean passport. If you do, this will be looked at as committing a crime if you use your foreign nationality.

Apply for a Korean ID

- You can apply for a Korean ID the same day you submit your pledge to become a Korean national

- You must bring the following when you apply for your Korean ID:
    - Current passport
    - ARC
    - 1 passport photo (3.5 x 4.5)
    - Completed Korean ID application form in Korean

- You will receive a temporary ID

- Your Korean Nation ID will take 2-4 weeks to process

Apply for a Korean Passport

- After you receive your Korean ID, you can now apply for your Korean passport
- You will need to bring the following to apply:
    - Your Korean ID
    - A Passport Application Form completed in Korean
    - 1 passport photo (3.5 x 4.5)
    - Fee of ₩55,000 KRW cash only
    - Your Korean passport will take 1-2 weeks to process; you can choose to have this delivered to you with an additional fee of ₩3,000 KRW cash only

1. Application to Recover Korean Citizenship: 국적회복허가 신청서

■ 국적법 시행규칙 [별지 제3호서식] <개정 2018. 12. 20.>

국적회복허가 신청서

※ 어두운 난은 적지 마시고 [ ]에는 해당되는 곳에 √ 표시를 합니다.

(3쪽 중 제1쪽)

접수번호	접수일	접수자	확인자	처리기간

신청인 **인적사항**	현재 국적		출생지(국가 및 도시명)	
	성명(한글)	(한자)	성별 [ ]남 [ ]여	사 진 3.5cm×4.5cm (모자 벗은 상반신으로 뒤 그림 없이 6개월 이내 촬영한 것)
	성명(외국명)	생년월일		
	전화번호(휴대폰)	전화번호(자택)		
	전자우편(E-mail)			
	국내 주소			
	외국 주소			
	예정 등록기준지			

한국 국적 상실 일자	년	월	일

한국 국적 상실 원인	[ ]외국 국적 취득 [ ]국적이탈 [ ]국적 취득 후 외국 국적 포기 불이행 [ ]국적선택불이행 [ ]국적선택명령 불이행 [ ]기타

국적회복을 하려는 사유

수반취득	만 19세 미만의 자녀 ( )명 대하여 신청인과 함께 국적 취득을 [ ]신청합니다. [ ]신청하지 않습니다.

1. 「국적법 시행령」 제8조에 따라 국적회복허가를 신청합니다.
2. 만약 국적회복이 허가되면 국적취득일부터 1년 내에 현 국적의 포기절차 등을 마치겠습니다.
3. 각 기재내용이나 첨부자료가 사실과 다른 경우 국적회복허가 불허 또는 취소 등의 불이익을 감수하겠습니다.
4. 신원조회 등 국적회복허가심사를 위하여 이 신청서에 기재된 개인정보를 활용하는 것에 동의합니다.

년   월   일

신청인
(법정대리인) (서명 또는 인)

법무부장관 귀하

첨부서류	3쪽 참조	수수료 3쪽 참조

1. Application to Recover Korean Citizenship – English Translation

WORKSHEET ONLY – DO NOT SUBMIT TO IMMIGRATION (Google Translation)

Enforcement Rules of the Nationality Act [Annex No. 3] <Amended Dec. 20, 2018>

Application for permission to restore nationality

Do not write in dark fields, and put a in the appropriate place in [ ].

Registration Number	Date of receipt	Receptionist	Checker	Processing Period

Applicant Personal Information				
	current nationality		Place of birth (country and city)	Picture
		(chinese character)	gender [[ ] male Name (Korean) [ ] female	3.5cm×4.5cm
	Name (foreign name)	birth date		Photos taken within the last 6 months
	Phone number (mobile phone)	Phone number (home)		
	E-mail			
	domestic address			
	foreign address			

Date of loss of Korean nationality	Scheduled registration base			
	year	month	One	

Korean nationality cause of loss

[ ] Acquisition of foreign nationality [ ] Deprivation of nationality [ ] Non-compliance with nationality selection [ ] Non-compliance with nationality selection order [ ] Others   [ ] Failure to renounce foreign nationality after acquiring nationality

Reasons for restoring nationality

concomitant acquisition   For children under the age of 19 ( ), apply for [ ] acquisition of nationality together with the applicant.

[ ] I do not apply.

1. Apply for permission to restore nationality in accordance with Article 8 of the Enforcement Decree of the Nationality

2. If restoration of nationality is permitted, the procedure for renunciation of current nationality will be completed within one year from the date of acquisition of nationality.

3. If the contents of each description or attached data are different from the facts, we will accept disadvantages such as disallowing or revoking the permission to restore nationality.

4. I agree to the use of personal information in this application for background check, etc. for permission to recover nationality.

year   month

Applicant
(legal representative)   (Signature or Seal)

Dear Minister of Justice

fees

See page 3 of the attached document.

2. Application Form: Written Statement 진술서

진 술 서

【아래 기재내용과 관련하여 충실하게 작성하여 주시기 바랍니다. 진술
내용이 부실할 경우에는 보정요구를 받으실 수 있으며, 경우에 따라서는
처리시간 내지 처리결과에도 영향을 미칠 수 있음을 알려드립니다.】

□ **외국국적을 취득하게 된 경위**(출생, 유학, 혼인, 이민 등 취득과정을
　 상세히 기술)

□ **외국국적을 취득한 후 외국에서의 생활과정**(외국거주 친척유무 및
　 직업 등 활동사항 구체적 기재)

2. Application Form: Written Statement - English Translation

STATEMENT

[Please give us the detail information for below questions. If the statement is not detail enough we will request additional and it might effect to your progress and result.]

☐ How do you obtain your foreign citizenship? (Detail as possible include birth, study, marriage or immigration)

☐ Please tell us our life in the other country after you gained foreign citizenship. (Please be as detailed as possible, include your relations in the country and your career)

3. Application Form: Personal Statement 신원진술사

■ 병역법 시행규칙 [별지 제50호의2서식] <개정 2017. 8. 1.>

신원진술서

※ 모든 사항은 빠짐없이 기재하시고, [ ]에는 해당되는 곳에 √ 표를 합니다.					일련번호	

진술인 인적사항	성명(한글)		(한자)		[ ]개명여부	사진 (3cm×4cm)
	주민등록번호				[ ]변경여부	
	등록기준지					
	주소					
	실거주지					
	자택전화		휴대전화		E-mail	
	미니홈피/블로그			트위터/페이스북		

직 장	직장명	직장전화
	소재지	

국 적	[ ]대한민국　　　[ ]복수국적(국가명:　　　　)　　　[ ]외국국적(국가명:　　　　)

학 력	학교명	기간(부터 ~ 까지)	전공학과	학위	소재지
	초등학교	~			
	중학교	~			
	고등학교	~			
	대학교	~			
	대학원	~			

경 력	기관 또는 업체명	기간(부터 ~ 까지)	직책(직급)
		~	
		~	

상 벌	종류	일자	사유	종류	일자	사유

병 역	군별	기간	병과	최종계급	군번	미필사유
		~				

정당·사회 단체 활동	[ ]있음 [ ]없음	단체명	기간	직책	활동 내용
			~		
			~		

본인·배우 자재산	부동산 (원)	동산 (원)	채무 (원)

210mm×297mm[백상지 80g/㎡]

3. Application Form: Personal Statement – English Translation

Personal Statement

Please fill in all details and put a in the appropriate place in [ ].

Serial Number

statement / **Personal Information**	Name (Korean)		[ ] Whether the name has been changed
	resident registration number		[ ] Whether to change
	registration base		Picture (3cm×4cm)
	address		
	real residence		
	home phone	Cell Phone	E-mail
	mini homepage/blog		Twitter/Facebook

workplace	workplace name		work phone
	location		

Nationality [ ]Korea	[ ] Multiple nationalities (country name:)	[]Foreign nationality (country name:)

Education	School name	period (from to)	Location of major department degree
	Elementary School	~	
	Middle School	~	
	High School	~	
	University	~	
	Graduate school	~	

career	Institution or company name	period (from to)	Position (Title)
		~	
		~	

	Kinds	Date	Reason	Kinds	Date	Reason
reward and punishment						

military station	by county	term	Class final rank		reason not required
		~			

		group name	term	position	Activities
political party and society	[ ]has exist		~		
group activity	[ ]doesn't existO		~		

self and actor / **property**	real estate (won)	movables (won)	(won)

4. Application Form: Family Relations 가족관계 통보서

국적업무처리지침 [별지 제8호서식] <신설 2011. 1. 6.>

가족관계 통보서

<table>
<tr>
<td rowspan="2">①
통 보
유 형
(※담당
공무원
기재란)</td>
<td colspan="3">국적취득 등 사건발생일 □ 국적취득(원인 : □ 인지, □ 재취득)
　　　　　　　　　　　　 □ 귀화허가
　　　　년　　　월　　　일 □ 수반취득(원인 : □ 귀화, □ 국적회복)
　　　　　　　　　 - 귀화(국적회복)자와의 관계 : 의
　　　　　　　　　 □ 국적회복허가
　　　　　　　　　 - 한국국적상실일 : 　년　　월　　일
　　　　　　　　　 - 한국국적상실원인 : □ 외국국적취득 □ 국적이탈
　　　　　　　　　 □ 국적판정</td>
</tr>
<tr></tr>
<tr>
<td rowspan="7">②
사
건
본
인
(※이하
사건본
인기재
란)</td>
<td colspan="3">등록기준예정지</td>
</tr>
<tr>
<td colspan="3">□ 등록기준지
□ 본 적</td>
</tr>
<tr>
<td rowspan="2">성 명</td>
<td>외국어(한자포함)</td>
<td>생년월일</td>
</tr>
<tr>
<td>원지음의한글표기</td>
<td>주민등록번호</td>
</tr>
<tr>
<td>성 별</td>
<td>□ 남 □ 여　　국적회복(취득)전</td>
<td>본(한자)</td>
</tr>
<tr>
<td>기타사항</td>
<td colspan="2"></td>
</tr>
<tr>
<td>주 소</td>
<td></td>
<td>전화번호
(휴대폰)</td>
</tr>
<tr>
<td rowspan="3">③
배
우
자</td>
<td>성 명</td>
<td colspan="2">국 적</td>
</tr>
<tr>
<td>생년월일</td>
<td colspan="2">□ 등록기준지</td>
</tr>
<tr>
<td>주민등록번호</td>
<td colspan="2">□ 본 적</td>
</tr>
<tr>
<td rowspan="3">④
부</td>
<td>성 명</td>
<td colspan="2">국 적</td>
</tr>
<tr>
<td>생년월일</td>
<td colspan="2">□ 등록기준지</td>
</tr>
<tr>
<td>주민등록번호</td>
<td colspan="2">□ 본 적</td>
</tr>
<tr>
<td rowspan="3">⑤
모</td>
<td>성 명</td>
<td colspan="2">국 적</td>
</tr>
<tr>
<td>생년월일</td>
<td colspan="2">□ 등록기준지</td>
</tr>
<tr>
<td>주민등록번호</td>
<td colspan="2">□ 본 적</td>
</tr>
<tr>
<td rowspan="5">⑥
자</td>
<td>성 명</td>
<td>생년월일　주민등록번호　국적</td>
<td>등록기준지 (본 적)</td>
</tr>
<tr>
<td></td>
<td></td>
<td></td>
</tr>
<tr>
<td></td>
<td></td>
<td></td>
</tr>
<tr>
<td></td>
<td></td>
<td></td>
</tr>
<tr>
<td></td>
<td></td>
<td></td>
</tr>
</table>

210mm×297mm[일반용지 60g/㎡]

4. Application Form: Family Relations – English Translation

Family Relations Notice

1 notice Type (Responsible public official description)	Date of acquisition of nationality, etc. ☐ Acquisition of nationality (cause: ☐ recognition, ☐ reacquisition) Permission for naturalization Year Month Day ☐ Concurrent acquisition (cause: ☐ naturalization, ☐ nationality recovery) Relationship with naturalized (recovery of nationality) person. ☐ Permission to restore nationality - Date of loss of Korean nationality: year month day - Causes of loss of Korean nationality: ☐ Acquisition of foreign nationality ☐ Loss of nationality ☐ Nationality determination					

2 Event copy In (below case copy popular material column)	Registration Criteria					
	Registration base Seen					
	statement	Foreign language (including Chinese characters)		birth date		
		Korean transcription of Wonjieum		resident registration number		
	gender	Male Female	Before nationality recovery (acquisition)		Son (Chinese characters)	
	etc					
	address			Phone number (cellphone)		

3 actor ruler	statement		Nationality	
	birth date		Registration base Seen	
	resident registration number			

4 wealth	statement		Nationality	
	birth date		Registration base Seen	
	resident registration number			

5 what	statement		Nationality	
	birth date		Registration base Seen	
	resident registration number			

6 ruler	statement	date of birth resident registration number nationality	Registration base (seen)

Housing

Cost of Living

The cost of living in Korea can be reasonable, however costs are more expensive living in a city such as Seoul. In Korea, one can expect to earn a livable wage and save some earnings without having to live on a tight monthly budget.

Highrise housing; Incheon, Korea; photography by Antonia Giordano

Other than Seoul, some other large cities that are more expensive to live are Incheon, Jeju Island, and Busan. As of 2022, it is estimated a family of four can expect to spend about ₩2,300,000 KRW per month ($2,000 USD) in living expenses, not including rent. If you are single and live alone, you can expect to pay about ₩652,000 KRW per month ($560 USD), again not including your housing rent.

Below is a look at the average monthly living costs for large cities in Korea according to Internation's website as of 2022.

Average Monthly Living Expenses for a Family of Four (excluding rent)

City	KRW	USD
Seoul	₩2,700,000	$2,300
Incheon	₩1,900,000	$1,600
Jeju Island	₩1,200,000	$1,000
Busan	₩3,345,000	$2,900

Average Monthly Living Expenses for a Single Person (excluding rent)

City	KRW	USD
Seoul	₩711,000	$600
Incheon	₩665,000	$560
Jeju Island	₩540,000	$460
Busan	₩690,000	$590

Accommodations

Your largest living expense in Korea may be your housing. Most housing consists of apartments and condominiums and are expensive; you should plan to pay at least 30% to 40% of your monthly salary for one to three rooms.

When you move to Korea, you will want to plan to stay with a friend or at a hotel as it may take anywhere from one week to a month to find housing in Korea after you arrive. The moment you find a place, act fast in securing it because it could be taken up by another would-be buyer within a day or two.

Typical one room apartment, photography by Antonia Giordano

Typical one room apartment, photography by Antonia Giordano

It's good to understand some basic Korean as it will help when it comes to renting an apartment in Korea. Watch out not to be misled by ads or given the run-around by landlords. In place of this, have a Korean translator with you.

Before renting make sure you learn the average rent prices in Korea. Renting or buying space in Korea is very different than in Western countries.

In 2022, an average mortgage will start at -

- A small apartment or a studio:
  - ₩1.5 - ₩2.5 million KRW , $130,000 - $215,000 USD
- A 3 - 4 bedroom apartment:
  - About ₩4 million KRW, about $340,000 USD

You can expect to pay about $800 USD a month excluding utilities for a one-bedroom apartment in the city and around $2,100 USD for a three-bedroom.

Monthly Rent for a Three-Bedroom Apartment

City	KRW	USD
Seoul	₩2,600,000	$2,200
Incheon	₩1,170,000	$1,000
Jeju Island	₩1,170,000	$1,000
Busan	₩1,170,000	$1,000

Monthly Rent for a One-Bedroom Apartment

City	KRW	USD
Seoul	₩818,000	$700
Incheon	₩467,000	$400
Jeju Island	₩700,400	$600
Busan	₩525,000	$450

Types of Rental Units

There are five main types of living quarters available for renters.

1. **Apartments:** The most popular type is the apartment, known in Korean as an "apatu" (pronounced ah-pah-tuu). Because many young adults live with their parents until they marry and couples tend to have children quickly, most apartments are two or three-bedroom units. One-bedroom apartments are not as common and as such are quite expensive.

2. **Officetels:** The second type is the "officetel," which is designed to be used as either a workplace or a residence. Many function as studio apartments and have modern designs. In trendy neighborhoods, they can be quite expensive. This space is small compared to Western standards. An officetel can run much cheaper than an apartment. Depending on the upkeep of the building, some of these can be very nice or extremely rundown. They are furnished already but you will need to provide your basic living amenities.

3. **Villas:** The third and least popular type is known as a "villa." Note that these do not resemble Roman villas! They are smaller brick buildings with eight to ten units. They tend not to be as modern as other options but are often quite spacious and are the least expensive option. Villas are harder to find in the big city, but very nice to live in if kept up well. They are unfurnished, so you will need to furnish them yourself.

4. **Goshiwons:** Another inexpensive option, especially if you are moving to Korea for your studies, is a goshiwon (고시원). It is a basic dormitory-style room with simple furnishings generally aimed at students. A goshiwon may not be ideal for a long-term stay. If you want to settle, and obtain an F-4 visa and/or dual citizenship, you will want to show a sustainable lifestyle and housing.

5. **Flatshares:** This is also common for people on a budget, and if you're looking for a flatshare, then the best places to search are Facebook groups and Craigslist.com. These may be your best bet for finding shorter-term leases as traditional leases typically last for two years.

Apartments and villas do not have long leases, but will usually be offered unfurnished while officetels often come furnished. Because of this, an officetel can be a convenient short-term option if it's within your budget.

Neighborhoods in Seoul

Naturally, your choice of which neighborhood to live in will be dictated by your personal reasons for wanting to move. Seoul does have a strong public transit system, which affords some convenience if you're on a budget and you wish to live further away from the heart of town where rent is cheaper.

Seoul is divided into districts, called "gu" (구) and subdistricts, called "dong". The center of the city is split from north to south by the Han River. The districts north of the river are homes to a lot of foreign or ex-pat communities. The districts south of the river are becoming more popular with young professionals and foreign workers. The Daechi-dong (대치동) in Gangnam-Gu (강남구) is a central commercial hub and the most popular neighborhood for foreigners.

How to Find a Rental

Many people use a real estate agent to help them find a rental. Here are some good resources for finding housing and approved realtors:

* http://global.seoul.go.kr/index.do?site_code=0101
* http://housingseoul.com
* https://seoulhomes.kr
* https://wise.com/us/blog/renting-in-seoul-south-korea
* https://www.internations.org/go/moving-to-south-korea/housing
* https://www.aetnainternational.com/en/about-us/explore/living-abroad/culture-lifestyle/living-in-south-korea-housing-types.html

Jeonse vs. Wolse

The Seoul housing rental market follows two unusual systems for paying rent. Landlords use the "Jeonse" system which requires a large deposit up-front and the landlord takes interest from the deposit in place of rent. The deposit is then returned at the end of the tenancy.

The second system is called "Wolse", which is like the American rental system. You pay a smaller initial deposit and monthly rent.

Some landlords use a system that's a combination of these two. Make sure you know which system potential landlords use so that you are not surprised by having to pay a large sum of money also known as a deposit that may be out of your budget.

Pro Tip: Be aware that many apartments do not have ovens, but they do have microwaves and stove-tops.

Buying a house in Korea

If it's in your budget and you anticipate staying in Korea permanently, Korea is generally a buyer-friendly place, and most houses are offered with a low-interest mortgage.

Traditional Korean Houses; Seoul, Korea; photography by Antonia Giordano

The process of finding and purchasing a house is not that different from any other country, but there are some extra requirements if you are a foreign resident. If you are not a Korean citizen, you are subject to the Foreigner's Land Acquisition Act which requires you to inform the government within 60 days of the contract being finalized. However, you should be fine with this, when you apply for your F-4 visa, because you will already be reporting this to the Korean government.

Utility Costs

Paying utilities in Korea are easy and can be done at a convenience store. Utilities in Korea will not add too much expense to your rent. You will want to make sure you save some money on the internet, gas, electricity, and water. Utilities will generally cost a little over ₩100,000 KRW per month ($84 USD).

Banking for Foreigners

If you want to live in Korea, you will need to know how to open a bank account. This will not only be mandatory should you be moving to Korea for work, but it will also be a great convenience when renting a home, paying for utilities, or even just withdrawing money from a local ATM.

Try to go early in the morning because most banks are open between 9:00 AM - 4:00 PM and can get quite busy in some places. Some large banks have 24 hour ATMs, but they lock the doors and require an ATM card to open them.

Major banks in urban centers have at least one on-site translator and have translated documents, but it never hurts to bring along a friend who speaks Korean. If you don't know anyone, you can dial 120 to get the Dasan Hotline or 1330 to get the Korean Tourism Hotline.

Open a Bank Account

You should not need to open a bank account before you leave. It is much easier to open one when you arrive in Korea. Some documents you'll need to open an account:

a. A passport or U.S. military card 여권

b.   Visa 비자

c. ARC (Alien Registration Card) or a (Residence card) 외국인 등록 카드
    |

d. A copy of your Korean address in English and Korean

e. A certificate or proof of employment 재직증명서

f. You will also need a Korean phone number 한국내 전화번호 for the bank to contact you with any questions or problems

If you are a student, you can ask your school if it has special arrangements with banks in place of a certificate of employment. Minors under the age of 14 must be accompanied by their parents to open a bank account and must have a document to prove the family relationship. Korean banks do not require a credit history or credit check.

Pro Tip: Make sure to ask about choosing a foreign-designated bank if you plan to transfer from a Korean bank to your regular bank! You cannot have more than two foreign-designated banks at a time.

Services that are offered:

- Debit cards are available

- Savings accounts

- Internet banking (this has the least expensive fees); you may need to specify as not all banks will automatically give it to you.

- Online banking; you will also need to ask for a digital certificate, which is an added layer of security required to conduct online transfers. If you lose it, report it as missing.

- Multiple bank accounts: commercial banks do not charge monthly service fees

Banks in Korea that Cater to Foreigners:

There are the banks in Korea that are used by foreigners:

- Woori Bank
  - A terrific bank with ATMs and online banking and also has locations in the USA. It has an increased viability rating but a lowered issuer default rating (IDR) in 2021.
  - Main: https://www.wooribank.com
  - English: http:s//eng.wooribank.com
  - Korea: 02-1599-2288
  - Overseas: +82-1599-2288

- KB Financial Group Inc
  - KB Kookmin Bank (KB 국민은행), a subsidiary of KB Financial Group Inc., is the largest bank in Korea as of 2020 and has an extensive ATM network.
  - Main: https://www.kbstar.com
  - English: https://omoney.kbstar.com
  - Korea: 02-1599-4477
  - Overseas: Tel. +82-2-6300-9999

KB Kookmin Bank; Seoul, Korea; photography by Antonia Giordano

- Shinhan Bank
  - One of the top banks in Korea, it is the second largest bank in Korea as of 2020 and has a large selection of services.
  - Main: https://www.shinhan.com
  - English: https://www.shinhan.com/en
  - Korea: 02-1577-8380
  - Overseas: +82-1577-8380

- KEB Hana Bank
  - Hana Financial Group is owned by mostly foreigners, with good English support and services, but doesn't have as many ATMs.
  - Main: https://www.kebhana.com
  - English: https://www.kebhana.com/easyone_index_en.html
  - Korea: 02-1544-3000 x8,9
  - Overseas: +82-1544-3000 x8,9

Hana Bank; Seoul, Korea; photography by Antonia Giordano

- Industrial Bank of Korea
  - Main: https://global.ibk.co.kr
  - English: https://global.ibk.co.kr (will automatically change to your preferred language)
  - Korea: 02-1566-2566 or 02-1588-2588
  - Overseas: + 82-31-888-8000
- Nonhyup (NH) Bank
  - Main: https://banking.nonghyup.com/nhbank.html
  - English: https://banking.nonghyup.com/servlet/PGMN0001R.view
  - Korea: 02-1588-2100
  - Overseas: + 82-2-3704-1004

Other banks you might recognize are:

- HSBC Korea
- JP Morgan Chase
- Bank of America
- Bank of New York Mellon

 ATM

Not all ATMs accept foreign cards unless they say "Global" but all main banks and convenience stores have international ATMs. Your card may also have fees if you use them with taxis, restaurants, hotels, or large stores. Some places in large cities will accept U.S. currency but change will be provided in KRW currency.

It is recommended to have an ATM card or Passbook (bank book) so that

Global ATM; Seoul, Korea; photography by Antonia Giordano

you can use non-international ATMs found in hotels, post offices, and train stations which are open between 9:00 AM and midnight.

Bank checks do exist but are not common. Koreans do not use personal checks. However, they do have bank books, which are like checkbooks, but they are updated by placing them inside ATMs or special printers that tellers have. Make sure to keep it in a safe place and report it missing if you lose it. It's a good idea to update it monthly.

All banks allow foreigners to have bank accounts, but they limit ATM access for three months, especially if you don't have a residence card (ARC). They require you to conduct the first few months of transactions via a teller. Teller transactions have the most expensive fees, followed by ATM fees (including fees for depositing money).

Pro Tip: Get your ARC-F-4 visa as soon as you arrive. It will make everyday life easier and more accessible.

If you're a student, you might want to reconsider if you need a bank account because you won't be eligible for a residence card. If you wish to use a Passbook to deposit or withdraw money from an ATM after the first few months, you will need to let the teller know so they can make changes to it to allow you to do so.

To use an ATM, you will insert the ATM card or Passbook into an ATM, type in your PIN, then make your selection of cash (현금), check (표), or a combination (현금/표).

 # Transferring Money

Some options if you want to send money to Korea are:

*   direct debit
*   bank transfer
*   debit card
*   credit card
*   Paypal

You can also use various apps, such as:

*   Wise (best rated)
*   Remitly (fastest)
*   Small World
*   OFX (least expensive)
*   Truefriend (Western Union)

Venmo and other cash apps are not available in Korea. Toss.im is a like service. Make sure that your Korean bank account is defaulted to KRW (Korean won). If you plan to transfer more than $50,000 in a year, then you will need supporting documents, such as a tuition fee invoice.

Wiring money from Korea to another country

*   Use a wire transfer. It's the quickest and most secure method.
*   Sending a bank check is the second quickest and most inexpensive method.
*   There will be a transaction fee.

Limits

Make sure to ask the bank about their limits on money transfers per day, per month, and based on salary.

Bank Exchange

Also ask about the bank exchange rate, which may or may not be better than currency exchange counters or the market rate.

> **Pro Tip: Word of caution, there are a lot of con artists in Korea who will try to get your bank information. Be careful!**

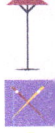

The Korean Language

Learning the language is important if you are considering living in Korea, whether for a short time or indefinitely. It is recommended you learn how to read the characters and how to say several helpful phrases.

For helpful Korean words and phrases, refer to the Adoptee Hub book, *Visiting Korea*.

Statue of King Sejong; photography by Antonia Giordano

Dialects

As you to learn Korean, be aware of where you visit and live as there are six Korean dialects. Sometimes this makes it difficult for people to understand your Korean depending on which dialect you are learning.

1. Geyonggi (경기도) dialect is spoken in Seoul and Incheon. This is extremely common and standard, especially when learning Korean. You will find that this is used a lot on TV shows, radio stations, news channels, etc. Many Koreans will understand this dialect no matter where you are in Korea.

2. Gangwon (강원도) dialect is spoken in the Northeast of Korea which is popular for having many mountains and forests. This is where the Pyeongchang (평창) Olympics were held in 2018.

3. Cungcheong (청남도) dialect is a commonly used dialect in many areas in Korea.

4. Gyeongsang (상북도) dialect is used in Busan, Degu, and Ulsan cities

5. Jeollado (전라도) dialect is used in Chunju and Kwang cities

6. Jeju (제주도) dialect is spoken only in Jeju-do Island which is on the southwest coast. It is one of the most difficult dialects to understand even for Koreans who are on the mainland. This is because Jeju has its own language.

Korean Language Schools in Korea

Korean has a handful of educational schools that can help you learn the Korean language full-time if it is within your budget and if you have the time to learn Korean.

Some of the schools we recommend are:

Ewha University: this is an all-women's university that has had foreign language education since 1988. This university offers a variety of classes four times a year that teach about cultures and languages. This school also offers to improve students' skills as global leaders while taking Foreign Language Programs, Korean Language Programs, and Korean Instructor Training Programs.

Dongguk University: is located in the center of Seoul in Pildon-Ro and was founded in 2002. This school has six levels of Korean language classes as well as courses about Korean culture and history. The university has well-trained professors as well as an organized curriculum. To start studying at Dongguk University, you must know your Korean level. Dongguk offers cultural experiences and a global buddy program to improve skills and extend understanding of Korean culture.

Konkuk University: founded in 1998 when they partnered with Ami Nafzger and G.O.A'L Korea to help adoptees returning to Korea. Since then it has grown to fill with 50 Korean language teachers and 800 students. The location is in Seoul on the green line when taking the subway. This university has a six-month long course to learn the Korean language. Also, the university membership program partners Korean language students with a Konkuk University mentor to help students study Korean.

TCCK Global Academy: this is a program for non-native overseas students who want to improve their Korean and/or learn about Korean culture. Classes are about 5 hours on Monday through Friday. This program offers general language classes and outdoor activities to make the Korean language more fun so you can learn quickly. Morning class contains speaking, listening, reading, and writing. The afternoon class focuses on K-Pop, K-Beauty, K-Wave, K-Kitchen, K-Culture, and much more.

Resources to Learn Korean

Before coming to Korea there are many ways to start learning Korean, whether it is to read, write, or learn how to speak a little. The following are resources you can explore:

Pimsleur

Pimsleur uses the scientific Pimsleur® Method, developed by Dr. Paul Pimsleur 50 years ago, which combines graduated interval recall, the principle of anticipation, core vocabulary, and conversation. If you're not sure, you can always try a free lesson.

Rosetta Stone

Rosetta Stone has been around for 30 years and focuses on the idea of immersion learning. It's been used by individuals, schools, corporations, and non-profits throughout the world. They offer a free 3-day trial.

Local Classes

Some may consider local classes to be the most effective way to learn because it stimulates kinesthetic learning, you can get better feedback, and you can talk with an expert one-to-one.

Apps to Learn Korean

Daily Dose of Language

This app provides mini lessons for a few minutes of your time. Lessons include a variety of topics along with vocabulary, slang, grammar, culture, and more. Mini-lessons are free, but a paid subscription can get you more.

Drops

This is a five-minute visual-based learning app to help memorize vocabulary.

Duolingo

This is a free website and app featuring five-minute activities to cover grammar, vocabulary, speaking, reading, writing, and listening.

Fluent U

Receive a free trial to watch videos that are captioned, get access to definitions, and get sentences with an image. It is provided for any skill level, and you have options of how many videos you want to watch and how quickly you want to watch these videos. It will keep track of your learning process.

Loecsen

Learn Korean for beginners for free. View words in Korean, romanization, and/or with an English definition. Words follow along with a drawing to help. Test your knowledge with a quick quiz. Printable sheets of vocabulary are also available.

How to Study Korean

This offers various levels starting from an easy level and follows 100 lessons.

Foreign Service Institute

Life Lingua has many Korean course materials from the Foreign Service Institute. It's great for beginners and offers 40-plus hours of audio and eBooks of dialogues, reading exercises, drills, vocabulary, and grammar notes.

Sejong Korean

For beginners or intermediate learners, this program offers speaking, listening, reading, and writing along with videos and eBooks that are free to access.

The Cyber University of Korea

This provides three-minute vocabulary lessons and detailed lessons on vocabulary and grammar. It has a PDF to print and MP3s you can download to help with studying.

KoreanClass101

Podcasts are added weekly. They also have a YouTube channel.

Talk To Me In Korean

They have 300 free video lessons on iTunes, as well as a YouTube Channel.

Easy Korean

Learn culture and language in 22 playlist videos. Videos show common scenarios.

한글

(Hangul)
- The Korean Alphabet -

Consonants

ㄱ	ㄴ	ㄷ	ㄹ	ㅁ	ㅂ	ㅅ	ㅇ	ㅈ	ㅊ
g/k	n	d/t	r/l	m	b/p	s	ng	j	ch

sometimes pronounced /sh/ (over ㅅ)
(silent in initial position) (over ㅇ)

구름	나무	아들	입술	무지개	밥	스타	안녕	아줌마	아침
guleum	namu	adeul	ipsul	mugiigae	pap	seuta	annyeong	ajumma	achim
cloud	tree	son	lips	rainbow	rice	star	hello	auntie	morning

ㅋ	ㅌ	ㅍ	ㅎ	ㄲ	ㄸ	ㅃ	ㅆ	ㅉ
k	t	p	h	kk	tt	pp	ss	jj

키	토요일	피아노	한국	꽃	어때요?	오빠	아저씨	오른쪽
ki	toyoil	piano	hanguk	kkoch	ottaeyo	oppa	ajeossi	oleungjjog
key	Saturday	piano	Korean	flower	How is it?	elder brother	Mr, uncle	right side

Vowels

ㅏ	ㅑ	ㅓ	ㅕ	ㅗ	ㅛ	ㅜ	ㅠ	ㅡ	ㅣ
a	ya	eo	yeo	o	yo	u	yu	eu	i
father		jaw		home		soon		put	seat
사랑	고양이	서울	겨울	봄	요가	만두	뉴스	하늘	집
sarang	goyanggi	Seul	gyeoul	bom	yoga	mandu	nyuseu	haneul	jib
love	cat	Seoul	winter	spring	yoga	dumpling	news	sky	house

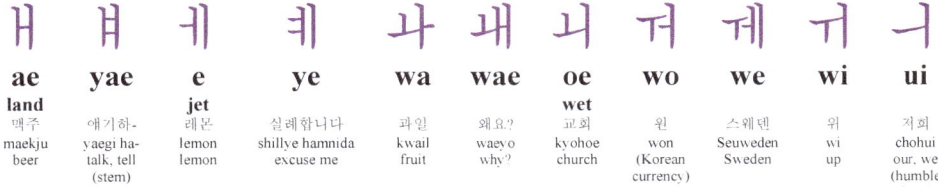

ㅐ	ㅒ	ㅔ	ㅖ	ㅘ	ㅙ	ㅚ	ㅝ	ㅞ	ㅟ	ㅢ
ae	yae	e	ye	wa	wae	oe	wo	we	wi	ui
land		jet				wet				
맥주	얘기하-	레몬	실례합니다	과일	왜요?	교회	원	스웨덴	위	저희
maekju	yaegi ha-talk, tell (stem)	lemon lemon	shillye hamnida excuse me	kwail fruit	waeyo why?	kyohoe church	won (Korean currency)	Seuweden Sweden	wi up	chohui our, we (humble form)

Alualuna / alualuna.wordpress.com

Grocery Shopping

In Korea, there are a lot of small businesses that own grocery stores or small chain convenience stores. It is more common to shop at your small local stores. If you are living in a large city, many times it is easier to walk there or take public transportation.

Before you go shopping, it would be a good idea to pick the closest grocery store to you and/or bring someone along to help you carry the groceries home if you have large or heavy items.

Pro Tip: Whenever you go shopping, bring your own bags, they are not free and there is a cost for each one.

Convenience Stores

- 7-Eleven
- Ministop
- Emart24

Convenience store, photography by Antonia Giordano

Traditional Markets

There are several outdoor markets that have an abundance of fruits, vegetables, and other foods. For more information refer to the Places to Eat section in the Adoptee Hub book, *Visiting Korea*.

Traditional convenience store, photography by Antonia Giordano

Traditional market, photography by Antonia Giordano

Traditional market, photography by Antonia Giordano

Major Supermarkets

Major supermarket have fresh foods and large bakery areas. You can also find some Western items as well. It will be more expensive. Many times you will find these inside of department stores and large malls.

Services:

- If you need a cart they, it will cost ₩100 KRW (won) to use, but the won is returned once you return the cart.

- Major supermarkets can do delivery to your home for an additional fee.

- If you go there frequently, you can get a membership card that will help you earn points and get discounts.

- Consider ordering groceries online and having them delivered. Most people use public transit instead of cars, and it can be a hassle to grocery shop when using public transit. Consider the distance you will walk, if it's uphill, and how comfortable the weather is when shopping.

- Most major grocery stores have an online version that can do same-day or next-day delivery.

Pro Tip: Be mindful of supermarket store hours, as many of them are closed on the 2nd and 4th Sunday of each month.

- Sales and promotions are common. You will see workers promote one product over another and provide free samples in hopes to sell it faster. It's not unusual to see a box of tea taped to a mug, for instance. Sales workers will try to sell you products even if you don't speak Korean.

- There are food courts in every supermarket. If you're hungry while shopping, grab something to eat.

Hyundai Mall; Seoul, Korea; photography by Antonia Giordano

Large Supermarkets

E-Mart

- E-Mart is the oldest and largest discount store chain that is also known as a one-stop shop for ex-pats. Even if you don't speak Korean, they will sometimes put mock dishes on display to appeal to their customers. E-mart does provide plastic bags but it's still a good idea to bring your own bags or backpack.

- Online: The online version is in Korean

- Known for: Tea selection

- Store hours: 10:00 am - 12:00 midnight, daily

- Address: 55, Hangang-daero 23-gil, Yongsan-gu, Seoul

- Nearest subway station: Yongsan Station, Exit 4

Lotte Mart

- Lotte Mart is Korea's top discount store. It's the most expensive grocery store and it is the most crowded. It's more like a department store and even has its own movie complex. Some Lotte Marts have aisles translated into English.

- Online: The online order form is not in English.

- Known for: Snacks and junk food

- Store hours: 9:00 am - 12:00 midnight, daily. Closed the 2nd and 4th Sunday of each month

- Address: 432, Cheongpa-ro, Jung-gu, Seoul

- Nearest subway station: Seoul Station, Exit 1

Homeplus Mart

- Homeplus Mart is the second-largest retailer in Korea and is known as a one-stop shop. You can also purchase Korean alcoholic beverages, ramyeon and other ready-to-eat foods. These are popular because of most Koreans lead very busy lifestyles.

- Online: The online order form is in Korean

- Known for: A wide variety of candy

- Store hours: 9:00 am - 12:00 midnight, daily. Closed the second and fourth Sunday of the month

- Address: 133, Cheonho-daero, Dongdaemun-gu, Seoul

- Nearest subway station: Yongdu Station, Exit 3 or Jegi-dong Station, Exit 3

Costco, Seoul

- You might be familiar with Costco already but it is very different in Korea. Because Costco started in the U.S., it also has U.S. products

- Online: The online order is in a variety of languages

- Known for: A wide variety of unique items and 16 locations

- Store hours: opening varies, 9:00 am - 9:00 pm daily. Closed the 2nd and 4th Sunday of each month

- Address: multiple, visit https://www.cochaser.com/location/korea

- Nearest subway station: multiple depending on location

Pro Tip: Tap water is considered okay to cook with and drink, but many people like the taste of bottled water rather than tap water. Consider this when you are grocery shopping.

Other Online Grocery Shopping Services

If you don't want to order ahead of time or don't want to go to the store you can order online. Some of these services are:

GMarket Global

- It is the #1 shopping site in Korea and the most popular among foreigners because they accept Paypal and foreign credit cards. Gmarket is a Korean grocery store, but it is easy to register online in other languages. A plus is that it has an English app, but the downside is that it does have several third-party retailers.

iHerb

- It is like an online foreign market but less expensive and with more variety. iHerb has an app that is in English and the website translates with the Google Chrome Translate extension.

SlowBox

- It is like U.S. community-supported agriculture (CSA) programs where you buy a variety of packages and select how often you'd like to receive them. They will accept Paypal and have great customer service.

Coupang Fresh

- It is like Gmarket but is less expensive. However, it's entirely in Korean. It will accept bank transfers.

Pro Tip: Most major grocery stores are incompatible with international payment systems. However, a website like "Wonderful" can help you place the order if that's the case. They charge 800 won/min with a 15% discount for first-time users plus an 8.5% processing fee that goes to the payment processor. Wonderful is a bilingual personal assistant service that can help with much more than groceries.

Food and Alcohol Prices in Korea

Grocery prices in Korea are fairly reasonable. However, sometimes you may be surprised to find that one of the most expensive items to buy is a bottle of wine. The following is an estimate of how much grocery items may cost. All stores vary.

Samgpyseol, pork belly, photography by Antonia Giordano

Soju, Korean alcohol, photography by Antonia Giordano

Grocery Item	KRW	USD
One-quart of milk	₩2,500	$2.15
One-pound chicken	₩4,800	$4.10
One dozen eggs	₩3,100	$2.65
One-pound tomatoes	₩3,000	$2.60
One-pound apples	₩3,500	$3.00
One-pound potatoes	₩1,900	$1.60
16 oz domestic beer	₩2,600	$2.25
One bottle of wine	₩16,000	$14.00

If you are not familiar with Korean food and its dishes, you can refer to our Adoptee Hub book, *Visiting Korea*.

Korean Seasonings

Most stores will have Korean staples like sesame oil (the Kadoya brand is recommended) or gochujang (red pepper paste). Other things you might find are curry powder packets.

Most stores will also have Korean ginseng, or hangsam, which enhances the immune system. The most famous brand is Cheongkwanjang, which is known for its red ginseng.

Checkout Process

Most people in Korea have touchless credit cards, but it is possible to pay with U.S. dollars in some cases.

Eating Out Costs

If you decide you don't want to cook for a meal and want to eat out, dinner at a cheap restaurant for two people will cost an average of ₩25,000-45,000 KRW. Dinner at a nice restaurant will be around ₩55,000-75,000 KRW

| Bibimbap | Dukgalbi | Korean Corn Dogs |
| Cold Noodles | Crab | Salmon Sushi |

Common Korean meals, photography by Antonia Giordano

Nuances of Korean Culture

Hierarchy

Knowing and understanding how to communicate with elders is especially important. Koreans will ask how old you are. This way, both parties can speak in respect to one another. Working in a classroom or business, it's important to know how to communicate with one another without offending anyone. Since we are used to calling one another by first names, Koreans have titles when talking to a person who is older or your boss. When eating out, the person who is the oldest is the first person to start eating and then everyone else joins in. The youngest at the table oversees serving the drinks and grilling the meat at the table. It is common to see people fight over how to pay for the meal. Usually, the oldest person at the table will pay, but after the younger person fights over the check, with the younger person showing how tough they are. Traditionally, and even now, the older person in the family makes important decisions and that is usually the final decision.

Hierarchy is not just around age. Whenever there are two people or more, there is a hierarchy that is built into the language. The hierarchy is sometimes also decided by gender, guest status, and location.

 ## Bowing

Koreans still bow especially when meeting for the first time and in formal settings. Korean adoptees and their guests may find bowing appropriate when meeting their birth family or foster family for the first time as well as for staff at adoption agencies, etc. The ability to be able to demonstrate some of the customs will be well received and leave a good impression especially when meeting someone for the first time, as you are representing yourself as a visitor and paying respect to the host country.

 ## Using Two Hands

When drinking with someone more senior in age who may also be your boss or mentor figure, it is customary to turn one's body slightly sideways and tip your drink back using both hands while averting eye contact. Usually, the more junior person at the table is expected to do a lot of the pouring of soju/beer/wine or whatever alcoholic drink is on the table. When drinking alcohol, Koreans traditionally have used two hands when pouring a glass for someone who is older and, in turn, while holding your glass when someone older is pouring your glass.

As a sign of respect, use two hands when receiving, giving, or offering something such as a gift, a plate of food, your business card, or a document. Think of it as a way of presenting to the other individual.

When in doubt in situations, it is always safe to defer to the most honorific or formal way and then you can always adjust yourself accordingly. Remember that the more you give to Korean people and they sense your sincerity, it will always be reciprocated and reflected 1,000-fold!

Keep in mind, most Koreans may know you are not native and do not expect this to be followed 100%. There is no need to be too nervous about doing any of this perfectly. You can always ask the person to show you how and no one will take offense. Geonbae! (건배) (means cheers, in English.)

 ## Drinking, Smoking, and Drugs

Using both hands is an important gesture to remember when pouring and receiving a drink. You would pour a drink if you're younger and receive a drink if you're older. While the person pours, hold your glass with both hands. While drinking, look away from the person who is older than you when they are sitting next to you to show respect.

Eating is customary when drinking, so buy at least an appetizer or two if you go out.

Smoking is customary, but there are often designated areas to smoke. In Seoul, there are many enclosed areas on the sidewalks designated for smoking. Remember, there are different expectations for women. Vaping is questionable.

Marijuana is illegal in Korea and the penalties are stiff. It is highly recommended not to try to bring any with you.

Speaking English

When you're in Korea, you will find people, especially young children from elementary through high school, will want to speak some English words to white people and sometimes even Asian foreigners. Even if it's broken English, they love speaking to foreigners. They also get excited when you speak some Korean to them as well, if they know that you are a foreigner.

Plastic Surgery

Plastic surgery is extremely popular in Korea. Koreans like and want to look perfect. They will get plastic surgery and it is very inexpensive. It's not uncommon for foreigners to travel to Korea just for the cosmetic surgery. There was even a Korean movie about a woman who got plastic surgery, dated her previous boyfriend, and got jealous of her former self.

Friendship

While in Korea, you will see same sex people holding hands, arm in arm, etc. This is how they express their friendship. It does not necessarily mean that they are in a romantic relationship.

Bringing Gifts when Visiting a Person's Home

It is a sign of respect to offer a gift or fruit to share with the hostess. Coming empty-handed is not an option. Buy some American gifts that you can distribute if you know you will be visiting a Korean family's home. Some examples would be a box of chocolate, coloring books/crayons, kids/adult books with English writing, makeup, etc.

Dating Culture

Having a significant other in Korea is important. It is common to see couples wearing matching outfits including shoes and underwear, particularly for hiking. Constant selfie photos will happen as well so that one is never running out of things to do while on a date.

There are holidays for girlfriends and for boyfriends. Valentine's Day is a day for girlfriends to give their boyfriend gifts instead of the other way around. There is also a holiday called "White Day" which is celebrated on March 14th. This is when men would give gifts to their girlfriends as a thank you for receiving a gift from the girlfriends on February 14th.

They even have a holiday for single people called Black Day on April 14th. On Black Day, single people will go eat jajjangmyeon 자장면 (black bean noodle).

 ## PDA a.k.a. "Public Display of Affection"

Depending on the neighborhood, acceptance for public displays of affection can differ greatly. It is not uncommon to see people of varying age groups holding hands, hugging, and sometimes even kissing at college campuses, pop concerts, movie theaters, coffee shops and on the streets. This gesture is slowly changing. Nowadays, couples or friends can be seen kissing or holding hands in public. It would be unusual though at other people's homes in front of relatives, especially when "older" people are present. Discretion is everything. Perhaps, as tourists or foreigners, you may get a pass, but if you do look Korean, the general society may not be aware of your Korean adoptee identity, so some cultural expectations may be placed upon you.

 ## Door Holding

Koreans generally do not hold the door open for others or strangers. If so, men go first. Korea is a distinctly patriarchal society, so unlike the U.S. and Europe where "ladies first" is typical, in Korea men are first. Regarding elevators as well, men will enter and exit first before women as well as eating first at meals. Some may be courteous, but not all.

Is Korea Safe?

The crime rate is low in Korea and it is one of the safest countries in the world. Theft and crime are practically non-existent to the point that if you leave electronics or valuables in public, they will more than likely remain untouched. However, low crime does not mean no crime, so of course always use your best judgement.

Safety

It is safe in Korea because Korea has an honor system. Even when it is dark out, it is very safe. When you're in the café or somewhere, it is common for people to leave their purses or personal belongings at the table while going to the bathroom or just walking away. If you do lose something, it will be put into lost and found until you come back to the place where you lost your item.

However, be aware when walking in marketplaces or walking anywhere, to be on the lookout for scooters and cars. Motor vehicles are frequently on sidewalks, which is a disadvantage for those who use wheelchairs to get around, but are cautious and will alert you to their presence by honking.

Getting Pushed Around

Korea's cities, especially the major cities, are no different than most bustling urban areas. Be prepared to be bumped or shoved through a crowd on the streets and in public transit. Remember, certain cities are more densely populated than any place you may have experienced and people can be impatient. Be sure to hold on to your belongings in the traffic jam of people to avoid losing or dropping items, especially if you have been shopping and carrying bags, boxes, luggage etc.

If you are bumped into do not take offense. Look around and try to find a safer place to stand. Blocking a path (even when unintended) may lead passersby to knock you around. Be aware of people who for no reason may collide into you muttering or shouting something. Unfortunately, there are people also in Korea who elbow others to pick a fight just because they can. It would be best to not engage, ignore him/her and walk away.

Shoes Off

When entering your apartment, someone's home, or even in some restaurants and stores, be sure to take your shoes off. Some places will have indoor sandals or slippers for you to wear. The reason why people take their shoes off is not only respect but because Koreans eat on the floor often and sometimes sleep on the floor; therefore, Koreans need to keep the floor clean.

Covering Sneezes and Coughs

Koreans don't cover their coughs and sneezes. When they do, they do it loudly.

Eating Out

Eating in Korea is a lot of fun. You will see many Koreans eat out a lot because it is inexpensive and reasonable! There may be a bowl of rice and kimchi at every meal, in addition to several appetizers. You will see people talking with their mouth full.

 ## Tipping

Korean restaurants do not expect a tip. Service is part of the meal and part of the job of the wait staff. If the bill is for a large party and the total is rather high, then one can leave a tip, more so in recent years, but it is not customary or required like in the U.S. If you are eating out with someone Korean who invited you, it is a given that they are treating you, and they will cover the entire bill. Let them take care of the tipping. It is not necessary to tip the following for their services: Korean beauty shops, taxi drivers and hotel bellhops.

 ## Leftovers

Customers asking for a doggie bag or a to-go box is very rare and if you do, it will simply be wrapped and placed in a bag without the carry-out container-type package you may be accustomed to. Koreans like to eat and enjoy their food fresh and hot. Meals are typically communal with the side dishes and are not meant for transporting home to reheat and eat "leftovers" in a small portion from the night before. Most restaurants will not pack leftovers for you, but some do, for example, certain brunch places and some Italian restaurants. It doesn't hurt to kindly ask but be prepared for whatever reaction you get from your server who is probably multi-tasking impressively to ensure the meal is prepared and served properly, keeping the true spirit of Korean dining alive.

Bidet Toilet

In Korea, there are three types of toilets: a standard, a bidet, and a squatty potty. In most public places you may find a standard toilet. If you are looking for a nicer toilet you may appreciate the bidet. A bidet is like a standard toilet, but it has features for cleaning the private area. You may find them in high-end establishments such as five-star hotels and restaurants. If you need help, some restrooms have emergency buttons for help, and some restrooms have etiquette buttons that make the sound of running water for discretion and privacy.

Toilet Paper

Koreans do not flush toilet paper, which can clog the toilet. Therefore, there will be trash bins to throw your dirty toilet paper in.

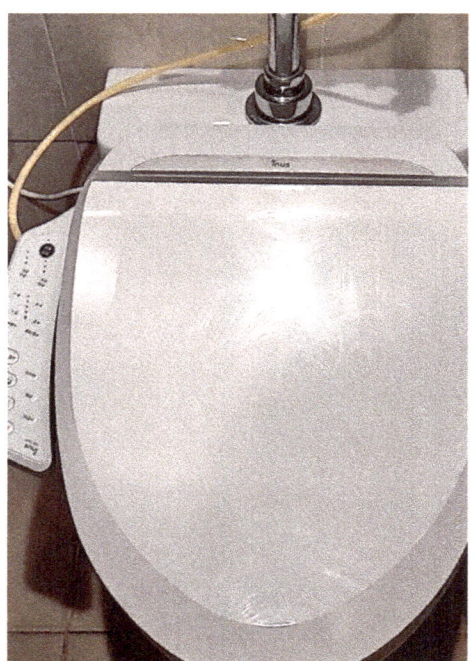

Bidet toilet, like a regular toilet, but with features for cleaning, photography by Antonia Giordano

Sometimes you will not find any toilet paper in bathroom stalls. Be sure to pack one or more travel-size tissue packs to bring along with you. You never know what you will find (or not find).

Remember to bring your own toilet paper and hand sanitizer, they may not be provided in public restrooms. In many restrooms, expect to see soap on a stick for the public to use, mouthwash dispensers, communal-use toothbrushes and communal combs and hair brushes. You are not obligated to use them.

Squatty Potty Toilet

If you are in the countryside and smaller public establishments you may find a squatty potty. If you are not familiar with a squatty potty they are toilets that are within the floor. When you use the toilet, you will need to squat over them. If using a squatty potty face the hooded area, do not sit on it. When flushing do not be alarmed if the toilet does not flush.

When going to a restaurant, bar, or café you will need to purchase something first, then you can ask for a code to use the restroom. Sometimes you can find the bathroom code on your receipt.

Squatty potty, usually found in more rural, smaller establishments, photography by Antonia Giordano

Women's restrooms may also have mini urinals in case a mother is accompanied by her son. If someone is transgender, you will find older-style restrooms are unisex, but note some restrooms do not have doors for privacy.

Pro Tip : When asking for directions to the restroom, you will want to ask, "Where is the toilet?". If you say restroom or another description, many Koreans may not understand you.

Getting There & Getting Around

 ## Arriving in South Korea

The Flight

When you board the plane, you will receive a complimentary amenity kit to provide you some comfort while navigating the long flight. This kit will likely include a blanket, pillow, slippers, sleeping mask, ear plugs, and a toothbrush and toothpaste. They also provide several meals, snacks, and both nonalcoholic and alcoholic beverages throughout the flight. Additionally, to help pass the time you can usually watch unlimited movies and TV shows or listen to a variety of music for free.

Before you land, an immigration form will be handed out by the flight attendant. Make sure you get one in English (not in Korean). It is recommended to complete this fully before you land.

Pro Tip : You may want to bring your own travel pillow for sleep comfort if you are flying in economy class.

Incheon International Airport, Korea, photography by Antonia Giordano

Arriving at Incheon (인천) International Airport

Upon arrival, you will notice that Incheon is English-friendly, so follow the signs and the crowd from your flight. Here you will provide the immigration form the flight attendant had given to you on your flight. You will then go through Immigration before you pick up your luggage. Once you have your luggage, there may be other things you want to do before you leave the airport.

- Pick up a Wi-Fi egg or SIM card for your phone if you did not arrange for an international phone plan before you left your home country.

- Withdraw or exchange currency at the currency exchange counter. You can also look for ATMs that have English as an option (not all do).

- If you arrive in the middle of the night when buses are not running you can stay at a Capsule Hotel in the airport. It is a short-term place to sleep and is a good option.

- The Korean spa is relaxing (but may not be so relaxing if this is your first time to a Korean spa). You can sleep at the spa and check your bags for an additional charge.

- There are many restaurants you can choose from if you are hungry.

Information desk at Incheon International Airport, Korea, photography by Antonia Giordano

Getting to Your Destination

You have several options to travel into Seoul from Incheon airport.

 Bus

Tickets are approximately ₩15,000 KRW (about $15.00 USD). Passengers will not have assigned seats. Tickets can be purchased from:

- Terminal 1, from the KAL Limousine counter next to 4 gate, 1Floor.
- Terminal 2, Go to bus ticket office (at ticketing office, Transportation Center, B1).

Bus stop locations:

Terminal 1: Bus Stop Number 3B, 4A (1Floor)

Terminal 2: Bus Stop Number 17,18, 19 (Transportation Center, B1)

General terminal information, Incheon terminals. KAL Limousine / www.kallimousine.com

 # Taxi

There are a few things to be aware of when taking a taxi:

- Seoul traffic can be very heavy at times and buses may be faster due to bus lanes.

- The taxi driver may know how to speak a little English, but it is not certain.

- You may want to have the address of where you are staying written in Korean to help the taxi driver understand where your destination is.

- Expect a 50-60 minute ride to Seoul. Your fee may cost approximately ₩50,000-70,000 KRW (about $50-$70 USD).

- Be aware that taxi drivers may try to take advantage of you by going on a longer route.

 # Train

There are two types of AREX trains you can catch:

Express Train:

- This train runs non-stop from Incheon Airport to Seoul Train Station.

- It runs from 5:15am - 10:48pm every 30-45 minutes and is located in the second-floor basement.

- Adult-tickets are ₩9,000 KRW, children's tickets are ₩7,000 KRW.

- There are service stations in both Terminal 1 and Terminal 2 at Incheon Airport.

- Payment by credit card is accepted.

All Stop Train:

- This train stops at 11 subway stations (on the Blue line) before it arrives at Seoul Station.

- It runs every 5-15 minutes from 5:15am - 11:32pm. Located at the airport station, in the Transportation Center.

- This may take up to one hour depending on your destination.
- Passengers will not have assigned seats.
- Stops include Gyeyang, Gimpo International Airport, Digital Media City, Hongik University and GongDeok.
- An adult ticket is ₩4,150 KRW .
- Fare from Incheon Airport Terminal 2 is ₩4,750 KRW.
- The Transportation Center is located on B1F of Incheon International Terminal 1 and Terminal 2. There are convenience stores within the airport and Tourist Centers (close to gate 5 and 10, located on 1 floor).
- Payment is by cash is only.

Getting Around

There are many apps you can download and use to get around Korea. Here are a few that are popular and easy to use:

| Naver Map | Kakao Metro | KakaoMap | Citimapper |

Pro Tip : Expect to walk a lot! You may walk anywhere from 7-10 miles each day, so be sure to bring some comfortable walking shoes.

Subway

The Seoul Metropolitan Subway is extensive and consists of nine lines and five regions, each with different fares: this usually costs about ₩1,000 KRW per ride on average with travel to the airport costing the most.

The trains and terminals are extremely clean and well maintained. When riding on the subway it is customary to speak quietly or not speak at all. Additionally, it is important to be aware of which seats you occupy as some are reserved for elders, people with disabilities, children, women with children, and women who are pregnant. It is also customary to offer your seat to these types of passengers.

During rush hour, subways are extremely busy and full of people. Expect to be standing elbow to elbow with other passengers for long periods of time.

Outdoor subway platform, photography by Antonia Giordano

Transportation Card (T-Money card)

T-Money cards are used for subway, bus, or taxi. They are reloadable and available for purchase at any convenience shop, within the subway station and at kiosks. The kiosks can provide instructions in English, but there may not be that many signs in English throughout the system. It is helpful to look for arrows, letters, and/or colors.

Korean transportation card, photo courtesy of Ami Nafzger

It is worth taking the time to review the map before even setting foot inside the subway. If the map is too overwhelming, there are plenty of apps you can use to find the right station.

For more information, including a link to maps of the Seoul Metropolitan Subway visit www.seoulmetro.co.kr

Pro Tip : When you travel on the subway you will have to scan your card to get past the turnstiles and to get on and off the subway.

Ground Transportation

 ## Taxi

When looking for a taxi and you do not speak Korean, you may want to hail an International/Deluxe taxi. These taxis are black with gold details. Most drivers will speak English in these taxis. The cost is slightly more.

If you have never used a taxi, and are having a hard time catching one, you can search for a taxicab station. If there are none nearby, look for taxicabs with their taxi light on. This indicates that they are available.

If you do not speak Korean it is helpful to provide the Korean translation of where you want to go. It is also helpful to describe your destination by using well known landmarks and names of subway stations. When saying a subway name you should add the word "yeok" (역), Korean for station, after the station name.

Pro Tip : Ask your hotel or the place you are staying for the address written in Korean, this information with help you communicate with the taxi driver.

Another resource to help you get around is the Kakao Talk app. For this you will need a Korean phone number. To get one, you will need a Korean SIM card (It is helpful to have your phone unlocked by your cell phone service provider before you travel to Korea.) You can purchase the Korean SIM card at Incheon Airport or a Korean service provider. You will use the number that is assigned to you with the card.

 By using the Kakao Talk app, you can request a pickup and drop-off location through the app, and you can pay the driver directly. Occasionally, the taxicab driver will try to call you (therefore a Korean number is required).

Pro Tip : Getting overcharged may happen. If you are concerned by this, you can report your driver. You can tell the driver that you will report them, they may lower the fee as there's a ₩250,000 KRW fine for overcharging.

 ## Bus

If you want to use the bus in Korea, it is both efficient and economical. It is recommended to use the Kakao Bus app. You can use the app to track your progress and help you figure out at which stop to get off. Just like the subway, be aware of where you sit. Some seats are reserved for elders, people with disabilities, children, women with children and women who are pregnant. It is also customary to offer your seat to these types of passengers. When riding on the bus it is customary to speak quietly or not speak at all.

People getting on bus, photography by Antonia Giordano

Trains

 There are four types of trains depending on your budget, comfort, or destination. To purchase a ticket, you can buy your ticket/pass online, go to a designated travel center, or through the KORAIL app.

Busan Train Station, photography by Antonia Giordano

Types of Trains:

SRT: Super Rapid Transit, it departs from the Suseo (수서역) Train Station in Gangnam, Seoul. It takes approximately 2.5 hours to travel from Seoul to Busan.

KTX: The modern bullet train connecting Seoul to other cities on five different lines. This train usually takes less than 3 hours to travel from Seoul to Busan.

ITX-Saemaeul: (ITX-새마을) The intercity express train. It is a little slower compared to KTX. Journey times are approximately double those of KTX trains and fares are 40% less.

Mugunghwa: (무궁화) A much slower train, the amenities and comfort are not luxurious, and the train tends to ride loud. It usually takes more than 5 hours to travel from Seoul to Busan.

Driving in Korea

Korea is a small country with a high-density population with little available land. You can imagine there is a lot of traffic jams, aggressive bus and taxi drivers, stop-and-go traffic lights, and lots of people. As a pedestrian, you should be careful as there are many accidents that happen because some drivers don't give way to people crossing the street. Some locals believe that those who drive are higher in status than those on foot. Also, drivers of larger and more expensive cars assume that they have the right of way over other vehicles and pedestrians. However, if you can get out of the busy city streets and into more rural areas, driving in Korea might be enjoyable.

Driving in Korea, photography by Antonia Giordano

Basic Rules for Driving in Korea

There are driving laws and rules; however, sometimes it does not feel that way. If you are going to drive, make sure you follow the driving rules.

- Traffic in Korea is on the right side of the road.
- The minimum age to drive a car is 18 years old and 16 to drive a motorcycle or moped.
- Cell phones are prohibited for drivers unless you have your phone set up on a hands-free system and use the hands-free tool.

- If you need to turn right at an intersection or at a traffic light, you can turn right no matter what color the light (even when the light is red). However, you still must stop on reds and drive cautiously. Especially if there are pedestrians that might be crossing the street at the same time. Pedestrians will have the right of way.

- There should be no drinking and driving. If you are drinking, the maximum allowed blood alcohol level is no more than 0.05%.

- Seat-belts must be always worn by all passengers and drivers.

Point System

Korea has a point-based traffic violation system. This means that if you violate traffic rules, in addition to fines or criminal charges, you will also get points. Each time you have an offense, the violation system has a set number of points, for example, speeding can get you 15–30 points. Getting caught using a cell while driving will cost you 15 points. If you get up to 40 points, your license will be suspended. If you accumulate more than 121 points in a year, 201 points in two, or 271 points within three years, your license will be taken away and canceled.

Driving in Korea with a Foreign License

No matter where you have obtained your license, from Europe, Australia, or even the United States, you are allowed to use your driver's license for driving in Korea if you have a valid international permit. International permits are only available in your adopted country. You will want to apply for one before you arrive in Korea if you plan on driving. When you are driving in Korea, you should have both your original license and your international permit on you at all times. International permits are only valid for a year and cannot be renewed.

How to Get a Korean Driving License

What if you don't think you need to drive in Korea until after you arrive? This may require more paperwork and be complicated, but Korea will allow you to apply for an official Korean driver's license until you decide to leave the country.

Korea allows for a driver's license exchange for nationals from over 100 countries. To exchange your license for a Korean license you need to present:

- Your passport
- A full and valid foreign license (not a temporary or probational one)
- Your ARC (Alien Registration Card)
- A certificate from your country's embassy declaring that your license is officially recognized
- Three passport-style photos (3.5 cm by 4.5 cm, taken within the last six months)
- You will also need to undergo a medical checkup that will cost you ₩6,000 KRW cash
- An insurance fee of ₩7,500 KRW cash

If you came to Korea without having a license and you wish to obtain it, you will need to go through the same process as every resident living here and take both written and practical exams. And while you can get away without knowing Korean when it comes to the written test, be aware that it is rare for driving instructors to teach in English. You will want to learn some Korean.

If your country does not have a reciprocity agreement with Korea, you will need to take a written exam to get a Korean license. This will consist of 20 multiple choice questions which are available in different languages, including English.

Return Your Driver's License

If you decide to move out of Korea, you will need to return your Korean license. To do so, you must go to the local Road Traffic Authority Driver's License Examination Office and present your passport together with your airplane ticket.

Car Insurance

Car insurance in Korea is offered by companies such as Samsung. For more information, visit https://www.samsungfire.com .

Renting a Car

You are allowed to drive a rental car in Korea if you are 21 and have a valid license with an international permit or a valid Korean license. However, finding rental car agencies that can provide all the necessary information in any language other than Korean might be tricky.

> **Pro Tip: Some companies are extra careful about new drivers. You might not be allowed to rent a vehicle or face higher fees if your driving experience equals one year or less.**

If you choose not to drive and are looking for general transportation information, refer to the Adoptee Hub book *Visiting Korea* which has detailed information on arriving in Korea and getting around.

Driving in Korea, photography by Antonia Giordano

Healthcare

In Korea, the healthcare system is ranked as one of the top systems in the world according to the Organization for Economic Cooperation and Development (OECD). The OECD is a unique forum where the governments of 37 democracies collaborate to develop policy standards to promote sustainable economic growth. The OECD is a reliable source that provides evidence-based policy analysis and economic data. Governments compare experiences, seek answers to common challenges, identify good practices, and develop high standards for economic policy.

Adoptees can use Korea's health insurance system, but adoptees are required to register after six months in the country. This is a recent policy change in Korea for you to be able to use the public healthcare system while living in Korea, rather than having to leave the country.

One downfall to Korea's healthcare system is the disparity of the number of medical professionals practicing in the city versus the rural areas. To experience good health care while you are in Korea it is recommend you consider residing in the urban areas.

Healthcare Insurance Costs

In Korea, everyone must pay insurance through their paychecks. The amount you pay each month will be dependent on your gross salary. On average, you can expect to pay about 30%, which is about ₩120,000 KRW ($100 USD) of your salary per month. These funds pay into the National Health Insurance (NHI) which will pay about 50-80% of your medical costs if you were to need medical care while residing in Korea.

If you decide to purchase private health insurance, it will cost you about the same amount per month ₩114,000 KRW ($100 USD).

Pharmacies

Pharmacists are allowed to prescribe and dispense drugs for outpatient care. You may need to go to a nearby pharmacy or drug store to buy headache or cold medication since they are rarely sold at any convenience store or grocery store in Korea. You can buy digestives, cold medicine, or vitamins at a pharmacy without a doctor's prescription. All pharmacies in Korea are marked with a Yak (약) sign and are well stocked with Western medicine. Most over-the-counter drugs are only available at pharmacies, but sometimes basic over-the-counter drugs, like Tylenol or aspirin, may be found at some convenience stores. Pharmacies are usually closed on Sundays, but you will find many near major transportation hubs and subway stations often stay open.

Pharmacy, photography by Antonia Giordano

Clinics

There are so many clinics located everywhere throughout Korea that you don't even have to go to a big hospital. The price is set by the Korean government, so it will cost the same at every clinic for basic services. A doctor's visit usually costs around $15.00 USD.

Hospitals

In Korea, there are over 3,000 hospitals that provide high-level medical services and are accredited by the Ministry of Health and Welfare of the Republic of Korea. Here's a few in some of the larger cities and provinces in Korea:

Seoul

- Asan Medical Center
- Chung-Ang University Hospital
- Ewha Woman's University Mokdong Hospital
- Gangbuk Samsung Hospital
- Hanyang University Seoul Hospital
- Konkuk University Medical Center

Hospital, photography by Antonia Giordano

- Kyunghee University Medical Center
- Samsung Medical Center
- Seoul National University Hospital - SNUH
- Yonsei University Gangnam Severance Hospital

Busan

- Dong-a University Hospital
- Inje University Busan Paik Hospital
- Pusan National University Hospital - PNUH

Incheon

- Gachon University Gil Medical Center
- Inha University Hospital
- The Catholic University of Korea Incheon St. Mary's Hospital

Daegu

- Daegu Catholic University Medical Center
- Keimyung University Dongsan Hospital
- Kyongpook National University Chilgok Hospital
- Kyongpook National University Hospital
- Youngnam University Hospital

Gwangju

- Chonnam National University Hospital
- Chosun University Hospital

Daejeon

- Chungnam National University Hospital (CNUH)

Ulsan

- Ulsan University Hospital

Gyeonggi Province

- Ajou University Hospital
- Hallym University Sacred Heart Hospital
- Seoul National University Bundang Hospital - SNUBH
- SoonChunHyang University Bucheon Hospital
- Korea University Ansan Hospital

Kangwon Province

- Ganneung Asan Hospital
- Yonsei University Wonju Severance Christian Hospital

Chungcheongbuk Province

- Chungbuk National University Hospital

Chungcheongnam Province

- Danguk University Hospital
- SoonChunHyang University Cheonan Hospital

Gyeongsangbuk Province

- Gyeongsang National University Hospital - GNUH
- Pusan National University Yangsan Hospital - PNUYH
- Samsung Changwon Hospital

Jeollabuk Province

- Jeonbuk National University Yangsan Hospital
- Wonkwang University Hospital

Jeollanam Province

- Chonnam National University Hwasun Hospital

Jeju Special Self-Governing Province

- S-Jungang Hospital
- Seogwipo Hospital

Injury or Illness

Korea Center for Disease Control (KCDC)   Dial: 1339

Particularly useful during the 2015 MERS scare, the KCDC provides foreigners with information about first aid and diseases in English, Japanese, Chinese, Vietnamese, and Mongolian.

Seoul Women's Help Hotline   Dial: 1366

Not necessarily English-friendly and not outside of Seoul, this 24-hour service immediate response line is for women involved in domestic abuse, sexual violence, or prostitution and should still be kept handy.

There is also a new service for women or children in need of help to indicate where they can go to a "safe place." Wherever this sign is in a window, women or children can go there, and staff will contact local police and escort them to their destination. It's similar to "Safe Walk" or some other campaign efforts for safety prevention in case of date rape, stalking, domestic violence, etc.

Emergency Information

These are some emergency rescue entities you can contact such as the fire department, the ambulance for a medical emergency, or the police if you feel you are in danger or see any danger.

Emergency Numbers:

- 119 – (they can respond in 16 languages) fire and medical emergencies that require an ambulance
- 112 – (provides you with multilingual translation) police
- 1339 – Korean Help Center for Disease Control (KCDC) (foreigner help-line that provides information about first aid and diseases in English)
- 1345 – Immigration (for simple immigration-related questions)
- 1331 – National Human Rights Commission of Korea (for questions related to human rights law and social justice in Korea)
- 1366 – Seoul Women's Help Hotline and Safe Place, open 24 hours to help:
  - Women who may be involved in domestic abuse, sexual violence, or prostitution.
  - Women or children can go there for safety prevention of date rape, stalking, domestic violence, etc. Staff will contact local police and escort them to their destination and ensure they are safe.

Adoptee Resources in Korea

One important resource for adoptees is G.O.A'L (Global Overseas Adoptee's Link) in Seoul, Korea. G.O.A'L is the first established, legal non-government organization for adoptees in Korea established in 1997. It is run by adoptees and provides the following services:

- Website: https://www.goal.or.kr

- "First Trip Home" tours

- Assistance with birth search

- Translation services

- F-4 visa preparation

- Dual citizenship and more

Outside of G.O.A'L. photography by Antonia Giordano

KoRoot Guest House: In 2000, this house was donated to the Korean adoptee community in Korea. It was given and is now managed by G.O.A'L. In 2003, it was given to and led by a native Korean to develop and serve services for adoptees. This guest house was renovated in 2004 to provide a community housing space where adoptees and their families can stay while visiting Korea. KoRoot offers a variety of rooms with free lunch, Wi-Fi, translation services, and a place to meet adoptees from other countries.

The price is $20.00 USD a night for a single bed, a couple's room is $40.00 - $50.00 USD a night, and the family room costs between $40.00 - $80.00 USD a night. To reserve a room, go to https://www.koroot.org.

Koroot: (뿌리의 집, 서울시 종로수 자하문로 125-10)

KoRoot Guest House, photo courtesy of Ami Nafzger

NCRC: (National Center for the Rights of the Child) in Seoul, Korea, is run by the Ministry of Child Welfare in Korea. They partner with the local Korean consulate in your adoptive country. If you are starting your birth search, it is recommended to contact your local Korean consulate to complete the petition process. This process involves filling out forms to request documentation of your records. More can be found here at the following site: https://www.ncrc.or.kr

Outside of NCRC, photography by Antonia Giordano

OKF: (Overseas Korean Foundation) in Seoul, Korea. This place offers grant opportunities to overseas adoptee community organizations and motherland tours. https://www.mofa.go.kr

Adoption agencies in Seoul, Korea:

1. **ESWS**: Eastern Social Welfare Society https://www.eng.esatern.or.kr

2. **SWS**: Social Welfare Society https://www.kws.or.kr

3. **HOLT International**: https://www.holtinternational.org

4. **KSS**: Korean Social Services: https://www.kssinc.org

Embassies in Korea

All the foreign embassies in Korea are in Seoul. Below is a look at some of the embassies.

Embassy of Canada in Korea

주한 캐나다 대사관

21, Jeongdong-gil, Jung-gu, Seoul

02-3783-6000 (in korea)

British Embassy Seoul

주한 영국 대사관

24, Sejong-daero 19-gil, Jung-gu, Seoul

Tel: 02-3210-5500 (in korea)

United States Embassy and Consulate in Korea

주한 미국 대사관

188 Sejong-daero, Jongno-gu, Seoul

Tel: 02-397-4114 (in korea)

Beauty of Korea

National Museum of Korea, photography by Antonia Giordano

Three Door Traditional, photography by Antonia Giordano

Haedong Yonggungsa Temple, photography by Antonia Giordano

Gamcheon Cultural Village, photography by Antonia Giordano

Kimchee Pots, photography by Antonia Giordano

Daegu Peace Bell, photography by Antonia Giordano

Dol hareubang statues, Jeju Island, photography by Antonia Giordano

Korean rooftops, photography by Antonia Giordano

First Person Narratives

The rest of this book is dedicated to Korean adoptees all over the world. These are accounts shared by adoptees who have moved to Korea to live and work. Their individual experiences are provided in the spirit of preparing other adoptees should they choose to return to their first country.

Many Rainbows

By Jane Jeong Trenka

Hello to friends overseas! I hope that you are well and I wish you all the best on your journey, wherever it takes you.

I have been living in Korea for about 17 years. I first visited Korea in 1995 when I was 23 and after I graduated from Augsburg University. I spent the next 10 years going back and forth between Korea and Minnesota. Finally, I decided that if I were ever going to learn the language, I had better just go and live there.

I'm not fluent in the Korean language, but I can function well enough to get along. I never had a Korean romantic partner, and I never lived with my Korean family, so I learned everything from just living in Korea or the classroom. I first took Korean classes at Inje University, then Geumgang University, Ewha University, and Seoul National University. I also received some private tutoring. I completed the NIIED (National Institute for International Education) scholarship program at SNU, which included one year of language learning. The program supported me financially so that I could take a year and do nothing but study the Korean language intensively. This was very helpful.

Sometimes when I look around and see how other people have married Koreans, I think that their lives must be easier than mine because they have someone to help them. I have had to figure out everything for myself. But being alone is "a rainbow inside a cloud," as Maya Angelou would say. I feel I am independent and can figure out things for myself. Maybe my skills are not as well developed as others, but I feel like I can do a lot of things. I navigate a lot of situations myself -- blundering through, but still, they get done.

I am a single mom. My child was born in October of 2014, and her dad and I parted ways before she turned one. That was not the original plan, but it happens. When I was pregnant, I imagined that my daughter would go to an elite international school, but that isn't happening now. I don't have enough money to send her to such a school, so she has grown up with other Korean children and has learned Korean in public school. This means she will have a Korean social network, and will probably always have friends nearby as long as we live in Korea. That's another rainbow inside a cloud.

Child's drawing, photo courtesy of Jane's daughter

Work

Like pretty much everyone else who is a native English speaker in Korea, I've done some English teaching in Korea, and I have done editing. I worked at Yonhap News editing articles for about 3.5 years, and I enjoyed that a lot. Now I'm working as an insurance agent, and I find that work to be very satisfying. It's enough to support my child and I also have a pretty flexible schedule. I work at Samsung and am qualified to sell life insurance as well as other types of insurance.

In my job selling insurance, I learned that there are friendly foreigners who are doing all kinds of jobs in every corner of Korea! It's been a lot of fun to meet them online and hear about what they're doing in this country. It is a hidden slice of society that I think would make an incredible book one day. Koreans would be completely fascinated by this.

My office is a 100% Korean working environment. There are a couple of people in the building who know English, but my computer interface is completely in Korean. The education to take industry qualifying exams is conducted in Korean and the tests are in Korean. Continuing education is also in Korean. Koreans say that insurance vocabulary is difficult and that even ajummas have a hard time passing the tests because the language is hard. But to me, it is all the same. It is all hard! So I just keep chugging away at it, no matter what is easy or hard for others. A lot of our insurance work also contains written Chinese characters, so I have to ask other people what they mean. I found out that many of my colleagues don't know these characters either. I often ask questions in meetings even if I feel stupid. Being a foreigner, I don't feel the same kind of pressure to save face that Koreans do. This means I can learn more than others because I do not care if I look stupid. I swear I have climbed the steepest learning curve of any insurance agent in the history of Samsung. I enjoy learning. There's another rainbow.

Being an insurance agent is not something that people dream about when they are little. It is the thing that people do in Korea after they have failed at something else and they are looking for a new opportunity or even just a lifeline. Our office is filled with insurance agents whose former businesses have failed. They don't like to talk about it, but I find out sometimes. For this reason, I look at all of those people as survivors in some way. Sometimes people have mental breakdowns inside the office because the work can be very stressful for many reasons, but luckily the person yelling and crying has not been me...yet.

When I told Koreans close to me that I decided to become an insurance agent, they discouraged me. They said that insurance agents don't have a good image, that doing sales is too hard, and that you cannot make enough money, etc. I just kept swimming, as Dory from "Finding Nemo," would say. Who do you think was the #1 agent in car sales and #2 in health insurance last month?

I look at my work as providing a valuable service for foreigners who prefer to use English. As far as I know, I am the only native English speaker who works in this field. I help foreigners immensely because I can explain the insurance products better to them than anyone else. There are Koreans in this field who can speak English, but I think products and policies are harder for them to explain, especially health insurance. A lot of people that I talk to are kind of kicking themselves for not having gotten insurance before. I only started my job about 8 months ago, so I tell them that they should not blame themselves. Until recently there was no one to explain it to them.

I see my workplace as a blue ocean full of clients. If you have a body, you should have health insurance, and if you drive, you need car insurance. It is as simple as that. I enjoy this job and one nice thing is, unlike a lot of other jobs in Korea, no one forces you to retire. As long as I can sell insurance, I have a job, no matter how old I get. And I enjoy finding all the needs that are specific to foreigners and helping them get those discounts.

I am also an adjunct professor at Sogang University. I teach writing and a course on Adoption Studies. I don't think I am a good teacher, but I hope that I can give my students a different experience. To be honest, I did not plan a lot of required reading for my students this past semester, as I wanted them to find reading to match their interests. Most of them enjoyed that and said things like, "This is the only class where we get to think about what we want to." Others hated it, but I suppose you cannot please everybody.

In addition, I do translations for the Korean Women's Development Institute (KWDI) from Korean to English. KWDI is a government-funded think tank. They produced and published the most important research on single mothers in Korea. The hard part about translating for one institution is that all the research papers are due at the same time, so when it rains, it pours. This summer, I could not translate as much as I have in the past because of my other work. I am still working on a 30-page paper that I should be finishing up pretty soon. I work on topics that are about gender equality, sexual violence, and so forth. When I first started translating, I was hardly qualified. A person was working there who knew that I was a single mom because we had met before through activist circles. She gave me the work even though many other people would have been more qualified because she was kind and generous.

Child's drawing, photo courtesy of Jane's daughter

KADs

I used to encourage adoptees to just come and live in Korea just to have the experience. I felt that no matter what happened, you would have an experience and that would be a good thing. But after the suicide of someone close to me here in Korea, I feel more cautious. I want to say that if you come here, you should also figure out what you need to do to pull the escape hatch in case things do not go well for you. Some people are held together by their social routines such as a job, or their relationships with a few close friends or family. What would happen if you left all that behind? What if you were in pain and didn't have that routine and those people to keep you stuck together and living life? What would happen to you? I think that is something to consider.

During the time I have been in Korea I have also tried to do some work for adoptee rights and the adoptee community. I keep up on current legislation and events peripherally. Though with all my work, my main priority is raising my daughter in a stable environment.

As for my daughter, she is socialized as a Korean and has no problem making friends. She goes to piano and art classes every day after school, which ends a little later than noon. We have private academies so parents can work! Sometimes my daughter comes to work with me because I need to work more and I do not have anyone else to care for her. But the moment she walks into the office, it is like a parade; it rains candy and money on her. People who take the time to get to know us are so nice to us.

Discrimination toward single mothers and their families

Unfortunately, discrimination exists, but that's the way it is, so we have to just keep swimming. People think what they think. When people do not know us they bring their stereotypes into the conversation. We have to deal with their lens and the ridiculous things they say, even if they are often well-meaning. I don't need to prove anything to anyone but my daughter. What I want to prove to her is that we can live with dignity, no matter what people say.

I woke up this morning at 5:00 to write this. Now I am going to wake up my child, get her to school, and go to work. Being a single mom is not easy, but I think it has helped me to create healthy boundaries and focus on myself in ways that I never bothered to before. I have done so much more as a single mother than I would ever have done had I not been responsible for a child. I certainly have done so much more than I would have as a married mom. Had I stayed in Minnesota, things would have been easier. In Korea, sometimes doing simple things is a struggle, but I know I am learning more living here. So many rainbows!

To my child, I say, "Thank you." To every hard situation, I say, "Thank you." Life has taught me this truth on my very long, never-ending journey to get back home. There is a rainbow inside every cloud. Perhaps this is cheesy, but it is also true.

Best wishes to you from our little corner of Korea!

"Go Back to Where You Come From!"

By John Ha

I was born around 10 AM. on June 6, 1966, at the top of a hill in Hyehwa, Seoul, South Korea. In my Korean family, there are five children. My sister is the eldest. After her, there are two boys, me, and then another boy. My younger brother was born on February 10, 1970, and my birth mother passed away shortly thereafter. I was then placed in a foster family for about eight months before I was adopted by a family in Sweden in the southern province called Skåne, Sweden.

My new home was in a small fishing village with less than 300 inhabitants.

I grew up there with a younger sister also adopted from South Korea. For me, growing up in a tiny village was good because everybody knew each other. I was a person with a name, not just the "Asian kid." The knowledge of me being different was always told to me by my adopted mother, which helped me to deal with people who told me.

John Ha, his wife, and son, photo courtesy of John Ha

When I turned eighteen; the age of legal adulthood in Sweden, I received all my adoption documents from my mother. I could have had them earlier, but she thought it was better to wait until I was more mature. She was right. I was initially more interested in South Korea and its history than searching for my birth family. In my documents, I found the names of all my family members including my grandparents on both sides. I learned later this is very unusual.

In the document, there were birth dates (some incorrect), addresses, and other valuable information useful for finding them. I knew what I had, but not what I could truly know.

I didn't think much of the information until a few years later.

In 1988, while in college, I learned about an association for adoptees from Korea, Adopterade Koreaners Förening (AKF). The organization was founded in 1986 in Stockholm, Sweden. A year later they organized in Göteborg, Sweden. My local chapter in Malmö, Sweden opened in 1988. I contacted them and went to their first official meeting. I'm a "talker," so I was elected as the Vice Secretary of AKF Malmö.

My involvement in this group prompted me to contact my adoption agency, Southwest Children's Services (SWS) to find my younger sibling. They told me that my brother was also adopted by a Swedish family. I contacted his adoptive parents and sent them copies of my adoption documents and soon after I received a letter from my brother. We met later at my home. He was twenty at that time.

In the fall of 1997, I got a phone call from someone who spoke Korean. I heard the name but pretended to have some problems with the line. I made some fake sounds and hung up. A few minutes later a female interpreter called and told me that my oldest brother wanted to talk with me. He asked if I could come to Korea the next day, next week, or the next month. I told him that I could visit the next year during the spring. I explained that I had no money. He immediately said that he would send me money for the airplane ticket.

On May 1, 1998, I visited Korea for the first time since leaving. I met my brothers at the airport, and they drove me to my oldest brother's home where I met my father. Upon meeting them I didn't feel anything special. A few days later I attended my cousin's eldest son's wedding. I met my older sister and her family there. It was then that my emotions erupted. She looked like our mother, and this made me cry.

Working and meeting adoptees from all over the world, and hearing about their lives has made me realize that many adoptees need help finding their birth families. I learned about and worked with Global Overseas Adoptees Link (G.O.A.'L.), in 1998, when I visited South Korea that first time.

In 2001 I was living in Sweden and working as the president of AKF Malmö. In this role, I was invited to the "Second International Gathering" in Oslo, Norway. On the last night at the gala dinner, I promised Ami Nafzger, the CEO, that I would come to South Korea and work with her.

She replied: "I have heard that before."

The next time I would see her was at G.O.A.'L.'s office in Myungdong, South Korea in March 2002.

I said, "I'm here now!"

She replied, "Who are you?"

This began my time living and working in Korea. While working for G.O.A.'L. I became close to a Korean woman, one of the volunteers. We started dating and later she became my wife.

When Ami Nafzger, decided to move back to the U.S.A. she asked me to take over for her. With my former experiences and my time working with her and the organization, she felt confident that I would keep the organization working. That is how I became the Interim Secretary General of G.O.A.'L.

In Sweden, I was a teacher, a leisure time pedagogue, so teaching came naturally for me here in South Korea. I started my own teaching business, where I teach English to private students.

I have a son who is now 14, and he is aware of my two cultures. It was a little bit hard for him to understand why his father couldn't speak Korean. His first language is Korean, and I speak English with him. We don't speak any Swedish, but once a week we take a Swedish culture and language class together with another boy his age.

The only obvious cultural difference between my wife and me is that I get stressed about being on time. Growing up in Sweden, we are used to being on time and to making sure we arrive five minutes early. Most of the time my Swedish culture and my wife's Korean culture do not clash.

If you want to move to South Korea, here are my basic recommendations:

1. Bring enough money to live for three months. During this time, you need to get your visa (such as F-4 or dual citizenship), find long-term housing, and get a job.

2. Take Korean language courses if you don't already know some basic Korean.

3. Contact organizations that support adoptees who can help you with translations, family birth search, social activities, etc.

Living in Korea can be hard if you don't have a strong sense of self. Have you come to Korea to escape racism? If so, be ready to face it here as well. I have firsthand experience. Several times taxi drivers have asked me if I am either Japanese, Chinese, Mongolian, Filipina, or Mexican. One time the driver asked me if I were Indian (in Korean it is "Indo"), so I said, "F.... you!" Of course, not all drivers speak like this.

John Ha, photo courtesy of John Ha

Once when I was applying for a teaching job at an academy, they asked me a lot of questions, but in the end, they asked me if I was "white." My many years of teaching experience were not important to them. After that, I said to myself that I will never feel humiliated again. I never applied for another teaching job.

153

You may not have felt accepted as a Korean in your adopted country. Imagine coming to Korea and having Koreans question your identity. Being rejected several times in your life may be particularly challenging. Be prepared and be aware that you will not automatically fit in because of your appearance, or even your language skills.

Having two cultures and being able to incorporate both into my life has made me see the importance of my work. I know how meaningful it is to assist and help other adoptees find their birth families and/or help them learn about their Korean heritage. In all my years working with the adoptee community, since 1988, I have come to realize that this work has become a way of life for me, even as it contributes to my journey.

John Tae-Shik Ha

Formerly John Tae-Shik Hamrin

Real Korea: Convenience Stores and Late Night Coffee

By Kate Powers

My desire to live in South Korea fluctuated for over a decade ever since my first visit back in 2006. I became skilled at coming up with various excuses that prevented me from making the move but over time my curiosity about living in Korea hadn't entirely diminished. Ultimately the thought of looking back on life with regret for not doing it became stronger than excuses, so I decided to do it. I've been living in Seoul since July 2019.

I intentionally decided to move to Korea with no concrete specific plan. I moved from the USA without a visa, address, job, support system, or time-line. I'd been to Seoul before I had no familiarity with it whatsoever. It was essentially an entirely new playground full of shiny bright things and obstacles. All I knew was that I wanted to travel throughout Asia and other countries nearby, and I wanted to learn who and what Korea is by experiencing the people and day-to-day life in ways that visiting could not accurately and completely capture. I wanted to create new and happy memories in Korea but mostly I wanted to live in Korea as a demonstration that I could and that it was a choice I could make just for myself. I knew people who had lived in Korea with many of the same hurdles I had such as not speaking the language heard about the fun and exciting experiences they had I thought, "Well, they had a great time living in Korea, I want that too. So, I'm gonna go get it!"

Kate Powers, courtesy of Kate Powers

155

Off I went to the mysterious motherland. The world was open. It was a clean slate…sort of. I did have a very solid seven Korean words in my lexicon despite taking Korean language classes for a few months before, a reservation secured at the Seoul immigration office (but I did not know how to get there and I had never used public transportation in Korea), and 30 days reserved at a guesthouse in Gangnam, from the song from Gangnam Style…simply because it was the only neighborhood in Seoul I'd ever heard of.

I didn't know what all would happen, but I fully trusted I would figure everything out. I didn't know that much about Korea, but I knew just enough to be aware of some of the cultural differences and challenges coming my way. Many may have found all this unsettling and crazy, but I felt alive, adventurous, and empowered.

As some of us have, I've too had a teetering relationship with Korea. My first visit was in 2006. I had recently discovered some severe health conditions that were leading to a permanent disability with no clear cause. Eventually, it was assumed by a mystified doctor after doctor to be genetic. This unsettling diagnosis and fear propelled me to find my Korean family in hopes of learning anything about my health history. While friends were settling into their first jobs after college, excited about "The American Dream," I was connecting with Korean adoptees in Yahoo! groups and discovered G.O.A.'L. and KoRoot. I arrived in Seoul naïve and scared of my small hometown in Missouri. I'd never eaten Korean food or had any exposure to it or other aspects of Korea growing up. The first two people I met upon landing in Korea were Dae-won and Pastor Kim. They provided great support and solace during this experience that was otherwise very distressing. Meeting my Korean parents and sister and brother left me with many more questions than answers. Learning about their lives and the beginning of mine is a complex topic swirled with layers of ache and sharpness, and a peace that has taken time and effort to develop. I don't remember much of my first visit but I left horrified and said I would never return.

A month later, I reconnected with Yahoo! groups, learned about International Korean Adoptee Associations (IKAA) events and searched Dave's ESL Cafe website for English teaching jobs in Korea. I was confused and torn between never wanting to return and returning as soon as possible to dive in deeper into this obscure land that was now even more mysterious and perplexing to me. People in my life didn't quite comprehend all this and there was a quiet expectation to return to my daily "normal" American life seamlessly. So that is what I did.

Three years later I had somehow mustered up the strength -- or insanity or denial -- to return to Korea. This experience was also quite difficult. In my two visits over three years, I had mostly sad and jarring memories in Korea, and I could not remember most of them. I left in 2009 and once again said I'd never return.

After nearly nine years, I did return. I had lived in Washington, DC, and Chicago since they were bigger and more diverse cities than my hometown. My confidence had grown from feeling worthless and unsure of my identity to strong and secure so I returned to Korea in 2018 and stood firmly on the land with peace about myself and life. I happily floated around Korea carefree, almost with my head in the clouds as if I was an accepted and revered character in some dreamy completely unrealistic K-drama movie (even though I'd never seen a K-drama). I left Korea this time and said I'd return.

The next year I was moving from Chicago to Seoul. I'd previously explored a lot about my origin in Korea but not yet much about the actual nation or entire culture. Now was the time. I flew to Thailand then Korea with my mom and dad for their first visit to Korea. The second day in Seoul some people were noticeably staring at us for an extended amount of time and I was instantly transported back to 2006. Old memories seared my mind, but I was determined this time in Korea was going to be different than the past. The IKAA Gathering began the following week as did my official residence in Seoul. I was essentially living at the Lotte Hotel which was just fine! After the Gathering, I went to Jeonju to visit an orphanage for the first time, Busan for a few fun rainy days, then I checked into my guesthouse in Gangnam. It was already a whirlwind of a great adventure.

Everything was fascinating and I had a very open mind about what and who I'd encounter. It was as if this was my first time in Korea in some ways. I thought, "Wow, I'm going to love everything and everyone I can here. Korea is different than what I know and grew up with but that's okay and I'm ready to see it all! So, what if I don't understand anything and so what if no one understands me or approves! That won't stop me!" My narrative had shifted since 2006. The memories of when I felt irrelevant and unworthy in Korea before were fading as new memories replaced them.

Then, within my first two weeks, I was denied taxis three times. It stung and I cried the first time with a combination of exasperation and stress. Welcome to Korea! By the third time, I was yelling out defending myself. I wandered around sweating, yet it appeared as though everyone around me was not. I wondered why I saw so many women with lots of white coverings of some sort on their faces. "Is this some fashion thing? Some sort of ice towel for the heat??" I thought. There were five cafes on the same street as my guesthouse and four more within a five-minute walk. I wondered if I happened to be staying in some area especially known for an excessive number of cafes. My visit to the immigration office was interesting as I confused not one but three workers when I attempted to explain that I was born in Korea and therefore Korean but also American and adopted. "Why does being adopted internationally confuse the same country that began it?" I wondered with frustration. I wearily stumbled back to my guesthouse and saw a crowd of people inside and outside of what appeared to be a popular restaurant. The next night I noticed it was bursting with people again, eating, drinking, smoking, talking. I wondered, "how did I ever randomly select a guesthouse by this trendy restaurant and all these cafes without having any clue?" The next morning, I walked by it again, not quite as delirious as the day prior (but still sweating!). And that's when I discovered this seemingly trendy spot was GS25 - a convenience store.

I spent many first days camped out in cafes. I'd have moments of being overwhelmed and amused by the smallest interactions and thoughts when ordering coffee:

There's no cream for the coffee? Okay. No big deal! I'm here to be flexible, I thought.

How about hazelnut syrup for a nice latte? Nope!? Almond milk? No. Up-Saw-Oh!…Saw? Seo? Huh?? Okay!! No big deal, I'm here to get out of my comfort zone!

What?? There's no bathroom? Oh okay, it's outside and down the street?? I just drank 3 bottles of water in 5 minutes because I'm sweating so much. But this is all fine. Really!

Uhhhh, there's no toilet paper? Fine! Fine, fine, fine. This is an adventure after all, and I am living it dammit!

No soap!? Wait, what? Where am I!? Why have I done this? Why did I move here? How the hell do I get back to that cafe? Was it left here or the next alley? Why isn't Google Maps ever working? Ugh, I'm sweating so much. Oh wait, is that woman over there with the white sweatband thing on her nose the same woman I just saw earlier by the cafe? Hmmm, maybe I should follow her! Or is that someone else wearing the same sweatband on her nose and the same shirt and pants? Where the hell are they getting these headbands? Is it a sweatband? I am so confused.

Kate Powers, courtesy of Kate Powers

Then I remembered I left my backpack and laptop just sitting on the table at the cafe down the street. I ran back fighting the urge to panic about my laptop computer. I was pleasantly shocked it was still sitting there seemingly untouched.

159

To keep things as simple as possible after that, I sat inside Ediya Coffee across from my guesthouse slurping iced Americanos like everyone else around me. Everything felt weird and easy and difficult. I stared out the windows and noticed many plastic surgery offices and women walking around with bandages on their faces. Aha, that's where these puzzling head/nosebands were coming from. I laughed for previously thinking they were ice towels for the heat. I researched the neighboring countries I wanted to visit. I applied for jobs teaching English and quickly learned my photo was required on my resume. I also learned that if a prospective employer called in reply to my application, it could very likely be via text, some at 1 am, and that asking my age, birthdate, marital status, and (more than half of the time) if I was half or full Korean because I have the F4 visa for Overseas Korean but with such an American name, were normal questions upon first contact. I was asked several times by several people why I respond to text messages so slowly. I had never been told replying in seven minutes was a slow response time before. I hung out at GS25 chatting with people from all over the world. There were tourists, students, English teachers, and local Koreans. I ate BBQ and pizza topped with cubes of cream cheese and mayonnaise and pickles. I saw parks with kids at the playground at 10 PM, sometimes without adults nearby. I went to Dongdaemun at 11:30 PM on a Wednesday and it was full of people young and old bumping into me every moment. The safety and vibrancy so late at night felt like I was in a dream. I wobbled into my guesthouse exhausted and wired at 3 AM with a small box of strawberry milk and some shrimp flavored chips, a sharp contrast from my steady bedtime of 11 PM and snack choices in the U.S. of A just one month prior. I felt like a college student wannabe, but it was great. I was learning a lot and having a blast.

I started teaching after three short weeks, but I didn't want to because I was having too much fun at GS25. I got into a rhythm of working and commuting and looking at Naver Maps every two minutes so I wouldn't miss my bus stops. I spent seven actual whole hours in one week in a bank trying to set up an account. My eyes and nose and throat burned daily, and I learned about the air quality and pollution. I started wearing masks. I was wiped out many nights and sometimes I'd fall asleep on my used pleather sofa at 9 PM or before. Koreans responded in complete surprise to that. "OMG, why did you go to sleep at 9 PM? You don't drink coffee at 9 PM? You need to drink coffee at 9 PM!" Silly me. In the US if I drank coffee after noon, I'd be wide awake at 2 AM! Their suggestion was starting to make sense considering my new convenience store-influenced sleep schedule...

Teaching in Korea was wonderful mostly because I loved talking to Korean kids. I was still sweating all the time and for the first time in my life, I didn't have central A/C and was told to open all the windows as soon as the A/C was turned on even when it was 92 degrees Fahrenheit (this was pre-pandemic). It was all short-lived though as I was exhausted and ultimately wanted to teach part-time. I was also working with clients in the U.S. so juggling time zones plus teaching full-time (and GS25 hopping) was hectic. Coffee at 9 PM was becoming appealing. The school was not a match for my moral compass, and after a shocking experience with this, I began learning about other horror stories of teachers and schools. I've had a lot of different teaching jobs in Korea since then, largely influenced by the COVID-19 pandemic and subsequent school closures. Interviews organically become some intriguing little research project or a mildly awful hobby. If the pandemic hadn't happened, I'd very likely still be working at what was my second school. Instead, I've had several part-time jobs in less than two years. This is not the usual course for foreign English teachers in Korea but it has widened my experiences. Questions about my identity came up in every interview and some were much more sensitive or simpler than others. Some interviews brought all sorts of questions asking if I was sure I am Korean, or which parent is not Korean, or how old my Korean parents were when they went to the U.S., and why they went, and on and on.

Cautiously, I started teaching part-time elementary school, and it was awesome in every way! I loved it and settled into it with ease. I was now drinking coffee at 1 PM and staying up at night later and later was pleasantly adjusted to paying 500 won (about 43 cents) for ice in my coffee and 500 for a butter packet at Starbucks for my bagel. I was meeting people from all over the world and making new friends, both Koreans and foreigners. I mastered getting on the bus in the right direction and skipped around Daiso (a large franchise variety store) forgetting all my intentions to be a minimalist. I marveled at the bakeries everywhere and ate more cake than I ever have in my life. I went to doctors' offices, and I was happily surprised about how easy and fast it was! I was also shocked to see gloves are more often worn when eating fried chicken than at a hospital. I saw people with their shoes off in cafes and restaurants, others with blue hair, and others brushing their teeth in school classrooms. It was all so fascinating. I spent hours in late summer 2019 during a typhoon over my first Chuseok in Korea scrubbing black mold in my apartment. Happy Chuseok from Seoul!

I went to KoRoot for the first time since 2006 and was transported back to 2006 suddenly remembering the details of the entrance and staircase but mostly remembering Pastor Kim. Although I could remember only a few moments of previous visits, I could feel how much I'd grown since then.

Here I was, navigating Seoul. I wandered markets with Korean friends and cooked food with them at their homes. I carried soap and toilet paper in my bag. I learned to stop using Paris Baguettes and Starbucks as location landmarks because there were too many. I was entertained and bewildered and enjoying it. I loved the kids at school, and I was no longer shocked when I was told to open the windows right after the heat was turned on. I celebrated the winter and new year's holiday — twice, with cake both times -- and that is when I first heard about the novel coronavirus, COVID-19. Then I started to hear some opinions about the virus.

"We can't go to this restaurant because Chinese people like to go there! They have the virus!" It stung to hear that. I saw signs posted on some stores and bakeries that said, "no foreigners allowed." It hit me in a deep way leading me to wonder why a country that chose to send away hundreds of thousands of babies to foreign countries for "a better life" was now denying foreigners. Meanwhile, the Korean government started sending masks to adoptees in the U.S. Young students told me "Chinese people are bad" and "I hate Japanese people!" Meanwhile, Asian-Americans in the U.S. were disgraced by the words "China virus" and we're coming together to support each other. It all felt ironic, surreal, and strange. School closed due to COVID-19 the next week.

Feeling exasperated and unsure when my school would re-open, I started traveling around South Korea while the U.S. was shut down. I admired areas including Nami Island, Jeonju, Gwangyang, Andong, and other places, sometimes not quite knowing, or asking exactly, where I was. I explored small towns, coasts, and beaches and experienced the rainy season in the summer. I loved it. Still sweating again! My school had been closed for months and I had more interviews for English teaching jobs. I was told I can't teach English because I'm Korean American, but also that I don't look Korean so I can't possibly be Korean. How does one measure "Korean-ness" appearance exactly? Once an interviewer said, "Adopted! Oh, you all had great lives…why do some of you complain? Why didn't you learn Korean when you were young? Why didn't your parents teach you Korean?" Years ago, these comments would've crushed me, and I probably would have apologized. Those days were long gone. Instead, I wanted to ask her how she thought she knew how our lives went considering she could not even comprehend why my white American parents were not entirely equipped to teach me Hangul in the 1980's (before the internet existed!). Other interviewers were sensitive and thoughtful. Some apologized and some said they wanted me and any adoptees to have good experiences in Korea.

Dizzy from interviews, I thought more about South Korea's history with adoption. Did Korea, Korean parents, the general Korean population, and/or the Korean government request or even encourage the parents who adopted us to teach us Korean and about Korean culture in our new lives that were far away from Korea? Did Koreans check on us after we left Korea and ensure we were safe and doing well? Did they support us when we experienced challenges growing up and as adults?

Kate Powers, courtesy of Kate Powers

I started teaching again. I was at a great school with great Korean coworkers, and we had fun eating hot dogs wrapped in sugary donuts and drinking cabbage juice together. I sang songs with students and learned Korean words from them. I continued to travel around and saw lovely areas such as Seoraksan National Park, Busan, Daegu, Suwon, Samcheok, Jeju, Gangneung, Seocho, and Yeongwol. It was all beautiful and fun. I no longer wondered about funerals when I saw people wearing solid black shirts and solid black pants and wore my black shirt with black pants, alternating them with my bright colorful halmoni-style pants (halmoni means grandma). I dined at the tteokbokki (spicy rice cakes) hole-in-the-wall and The Original Pancake House regularly. I made songpyeon (small rice cakes) and skipped around Costco looking for pumpkin pies and turkey. I marveled at palaces and twirled around in a hanbok (Korean dress). I watched TV and the news, trying to decipher and follow along. I understood more about Korea than when I arrived and, although much was still perplexing, I felt very content overall and the height of the pandemic seemed behind us.

2021 brought another year of two new year celebrations – again with more cake! – and hope that we would have respite after the unsteady 2020. I played Yut Nori (a Korean New Year board game). I discovered there are things I appreciate greatly in Korea (safety and easy travel) and things I still really don't like (last-minute plans/changes and beauty standards). The inability to communicate with 95 percent of everyone around me has made peaceful clueless experiences and frustrating ones, sometimes both in the same hour. It all has expanded my understanding and misunderstanding of people. Although I've gone most of my life without the answers that I used to want many years ago, I discovered new questions arose from living here, about culture, Korea's adoption system both then and now, and social knowledge of that in Korea. I've encountered a lot of Koreans who don't know anything about adoptees or how many of us exist and I'd like to see a greater acknowledgment of adoptees. Living here has been the best way for me to see the realities of Korea and reflect on how some of these are related to adoption directly or indirectly. I've lived in Korea through my culturally American lens and that way is all I've known to be. This can cause cultural friction at times but, unlike during previous visits over 15 years ago, I no longer feel wrong for the facts of who I am. I was born in Korea and grew up in America with white Americans and, therefore, have an American mind. I'm not sure how I could realistically be expected to be any different. I've seen I can completely adapt without some of the conveniences of the U.S. but I also miss them a lot sometimes. It is the first time in my life that I've felt so different and the same from anyone at the same time. I've seen juxtaposition in both the physical and emotional realm -- old and new, compassion and anger, shiny and shabby, joy and disgust -- in myself and my surroundings. I've traveled wide and have seen the edges of the motherland and the mountains. I've been surrounded by people with whom I have a shared lineage but not culture. I have lived in this country despite being both celebrated and shunned by the only people on the planet in which I share a race and roots. I've been disappointed too because living in Korea is not just a curated vacation or fairy-tale but has been an immersion with Korean landlords, employers, coworkers, civil workers, and so on. It is not always comfortable for me to live in Korea but it is always empowering. Above all, living in Korea has affirmed that I am whole and complete as I am -- with or without answers. I didn't choose the beginning of my life but I certainly have the pen in my hand for the rest of the chapters. And that fact will always be a happy memory of my time living here indeed.

Kate Powers, courtesy of Kate Powers

Lessons Learned: Getting Educated in South Korea

By Madds Nielsen

It all begins with language

It was the summer of 1994 when I returned to South Korea for the third time with a half-hatched plan to study Korean for six months. I only had a vague idea of how I was going to proceed, no details, just the notion I was going to learn Korean. I was under the delusion that I would make great strides studying hard and picking up the language like a sponge. Earlier that year, I had failed admission to Korean Studies at the University of Copenhagen and was looking for ways to improve my chances of getting accepted the following year. Like a godsend, an opportunity to volunteer at an orphanage presented itself. A friend of some family friends ran an orphanage in Sadangdong named Sang Rok Boyug-won (상록 보육원), which translates to Evergreen Nursery School. I was going to teach English to the children and learn Korean the "natural" way. The orphanage became my first site of language instruction in Korea. However, this would not be my first time studying Korean since I already had spent some time taking private lessons back in Denmark from a Mr. Rim. Back then, none of the language institutes offered Korean classes because Korea was barely on the map of the general public's consciousness. However, one of the institutes was kind enough to provide me with the phone number of Mr. Rim and suggested I contact him for private lessons. Progress was slow, but I learned to read and pronounce hangul fairly well. I learned some basic words and phrases and became able to spell out those with which I was less familiar. This limited knowledge of Korean was a tremendous help for my self-study during my stay at the orphanage. Every day was an opportunity to practice and study Korean with the children and the staff that was working at Sang Rok, while studying grammar, vocabulary, and reading from a textbook on my own and with the help from the kids. This became my foundation for further, more formal academic language study.

Ewha Woman's University

I enrolled in Korean classes at Ewha Language Center which is in the university hub known as Shinchon, north of the river. In this area, three of the most prestigious universities in Korea are situated: Yonsei University, Sogang University, and Ewha Woman's University, and all three have great language programs. I picked Ewha Language Center because it was the cheapest, and I only had to go three days a week as opposed to Sogang and Yonsei, which had classes every day. This gave me time to work part-time, which enabled me to pay for tuition and sustain a life in South Korea. Back then tutoring English privately was an easy and quite profitable way to make a living. Foreigners, especially British- or American-looking ones, had no problems finding work. It was more difficult for kyopos (expatriates) and adoptees to land the best deals, but that is not to say that it was impossible. If you wanted to be a tutor, the opportunity was there, and the diligent ones could make a lot easily and fast. Koreans were prejudiced against their own when it came to English education, and it was not entirely unwarranted. English education was big business, even more than it is today. A lot of hagwon (private language institutes) owners were cheating and lying to their clients, pretending they were fluent in English or were qualified to run a hagwon when in reality they were just running their mouths and had no understanding of English. But that is just half the story.

Madds Nielsen, photo courtesy of Madds Nielsen

The average Korean was ignorant of the world outside of South Korea, despite the 1988 Olympics. It had been even worse before the event thanks to the dictatorship which had kept the population busy, oppressed, and indoctrinated. There was still a considerable number of Koreans who had never seen, let alone met, a foreigner. Of course, the people who lived in proximity to the American military bases would have been acquainted with the presence of U.S. Army personnel. Besides the military, white English teachers were most likely to be a Korean's first encounter with a foreigner in Korea at that time. It was not surprising that the average Korean would think that anyone with a white face was American. Fun fact: when a Korean would see a white person, they would not refer to them as foreigners but as American (미국 사람) . Kids would point and yell to their parents "American! American!" A white foreign national was synonymous with America even if the person might have been Russian, British, or Danish. Of course, there were pockets where "exposure" to "Americans" was more common than other places: Itaewon, Shinchon, Hongdae, Shinsadong, and Kangnam were such places in Seoul. Itaewon was right next to Yongsan Army base, the other places where hagwons were thriving. It was a time when I could support myself and my Korean studies with a minimum of work and still have enough time and money to have fun. The only problem was obtaining a visa.

Studying Korean at a university such as Ewha Language Center meant that you were eligible to apply for a student visa, which could be extended every three months without having to leave the country as long as you were enrolled in classes. Without a visa, you would have to leave South Korea and return which was a bit of a hassle if you didn't have time or money to travel. A popular way of resetting one's term of sojourn was to go to Japan for a couple of hours or a day and then return to South Korea. The cheapest solution was to take the ferry from Busan to Fukuoka, but it was also the most time-consuming for people living in Seoul. First, you would have to take the train to Busan, and depending on the type of train, that trip could last a good 5 hours. Back then, we didn't have the luxury bullet train (KTX). It was either the slowest and oldest train, the Mugunghwa, or the standard train, the Saemaul, which is about an hour faster than Mugunghwa. Today, traveling to Busan by train takes less time and is much more comfortable on KTX. You also had the choice of flying to Busan, which only took 50 minutes, but it was a more expensive choice. The least complicated but also most expensive option was buying a roundtrip plane ticket to Fukuoka. You could return to South Korea on the same day, but you had to have been out of the country for a certain number of hours before immigration would allow you back in. I made two such visa runs. I did not have the luxury of the F-4 visa since it would be years before the idea of a special visa for adoptees and overseas Koreans was conceived and realized.

On both trips, I went to Fukuoka. The first time was no more than an uneventful trip to the airport where I waited several hours for my flight back. I had just wanted to get it over and done with. I had no intention of taking advantage of the opportunity to travel and see the sights. My second trip to Fukuoka was the last visa run I ever made. I had to leave the country to get my student visa from Ewha University's language center. On that trip, however, I took my time and spent the weekend there, sleeping in one of those capsule hotels for the first and last time. Back then, the student visa was a big deal, and it was an incentive to study Korean in a formal setting. It felt like a game-changer, and studying gave me a sense of purpose, which running around town playing English tutor did not. Today, a student visa does not seem like something special for OAKs (Overseas Adopted Koreans). Many of us can now choose between the F-4 visa or dual citizenship, not a bad deal for newcomers who want to settle down in South Korea or simply sojourn here for a longer period.

Yong In University: B.A. in Physical Education

Learning Korean opened a new door for me; I was afforded the opportunity of going to college in South Korea. My friend and I were the first two foreigners to enroll as undergraduate students in the College of Martial Arts at the famous/notorious Yong In University, located just outside of Seoul. It is known for its Judo and Tae Kwon Do departments which have produced some of the best athletes in South Korea. It also has the less flattering nickname, "gangster university," because many of its students graduated to a life of gangsters. At least, that was its long-established reputation at the time, and it was well-earned. The atmosphere was the roughest and toughest of a university I have ever experienced. However, it must be said, most students were far from being gangster material, many of them were tough but kind.

The university has undergone drastic changes over the years. A lot of effort has been spent on changing its image from being purely a sports college to a reliable educational institution of high standards that appeals to the common Korean. Admitting students from overseas into their programs as part of the effort to change their image and promote the

university abroad as well as domestically.

These circumstances made it possible for my friend and me to study physical education at Yong In University as the first foreigners ever admitted into its College of Martial Arts majoring in Tae Kwon Do. Of course, the fact that I was connected did not hurt. On the contrary, personal connections in Korea (nepotism, if you like) were, and to some extent still is, the way to get around in Korea. Networking and knowing people are immensely important for newcomers who want to settle down for good or a couple of years. The culture shock, however, is probably not as intense now as it was in the 1990s. But I digress. I was fortunate enough to train and learn Tae Kwon Do from one of the most experts in the world, Dr. Capener. He was a Pan Am Gold medalist and a longtime resident. He also played a significant role in getting me into Yong In University and catapulting my future into life in academia.

I had no idea what I had gotten myself into, but I liked it. It was challenging from the first step onwards. Passing the scrutiny of my documents was not without its trials nor was exposure to Korean culture, not to mention the culture of Yong In University. The tone was authoritative and direct. Euphemisms and the mincing of words were not part of daily communication. At the College of Martial Arts, the tone and discipline were informed by the Korean neo-Confucian ways of maintaining law and order within a strict hierarchical structure based on seniority in which college seniors acted as the keepers of order and discipline. The way the hierarchy works is that every college student is given a student number, or a hakbun (학번), upon enrollment. The lower the number, the more seniority. The structure was very militaristic, meaning punishment was collective. If the professors or the seniors, for some reason, weren't satisfied with something, then the punishment was measured out to the class as a whole. Punishment varied from verbal to corporeal according to the level of egregiousness. The severity of corporal punishment also differed in degrees from push-ups to being battered. Yong In University was one of the last universities where hitting students was legal within a disciplinary context. Fortunately for me, being a foreigner, I was spared the harshest of measures, but l was not exempt from other humiliating though less violent disciplinary punishments.   Disciplining, however, was not an everyday event. Most days went by without major incidents of friction. The bulk of my time was focused on studying late into the night.

There are two types of students in South Korea: the ones who apply themselves and those who party or float through college. I kept company with the former. As a student assisting one of our major professors, slacking was not an option.

When we weren't taking classes or in the gym, most of our time was spent in our professor's office studying and doing other less academic-related stuff, like teaching my friend the meaning of the saying "all play and no work makes Jack a dull boy." It's not unusual for college students in South Korea to study during the day and have soju, play video games, and eat junk food late into the night, every night, sleeping only a few hours before going to class the next day. My diet during college consisted of chicken and pizza nearly every day.

When it came to studying, this period was the most difficult in terms of following the lectures. All classes were in Korean except for my mandatory English language class. The Korean I had learned at Ewha Language Center was useful but not enough. In every class, I had to navigate through specialized nomenclature, a lot of new vocabulary, and academic language, which most Koreans normally do not use in everyday conversations. To understand the subject matter, I spent a lot of time manually looking words up in the dictionary. There were no electronic dictionaries, and the smartphone had not yet been invented. Not only was I studying nutrition, physiology, and sports medicine, I was studying Korean as well. That is an important factor to consider if you are thinking about attending college or graduate school in Korea. Learn the language and study in advance the Korean nomenclature that pertains to your field of study. Moreover, make sure that you study a subject that you have a passion for because you will need the motivation when going through a sea of new, seemingly endless glossaries. Being persistent pays off. One day you will have the credits you need to graduate. However, I had an additional challenge to face: my thesis. For me to graduate, I had to write my B.A. thesis: the single most arduous piece of writing I have ever done in Korean. It took me an extra semester to finish, but I wrote it, handed it in, and graduated.

Sogang University: M.A. and Ph.D. in English Language and Literature

After graduating college, I got a job selling sports equipment in a shop located next to Kukkiwon, the headquarters of the World Taekwondo Federation (as it was known back then) where I worked for about a year before starting work at G.O.A.'L. as the director of Adoption Services. I did not have a plan to get a master's degree at the time, but I was getting increasingly into poetry. It was through poetry that I developed an interest in English literature, which culminated in my enrollment at Sogang University Graduate School in 2004.

It may seem strange for one to study English literature in Korea instead of going to the U.K. or the U.S. The heart of the matter was I did not want to leave Korea. I had built a life here and had no interest in going overseas to study. Owing to the F-4 visa, sojourning in Korea indefinitely had become significantly less of an ordeal. The way I saw it, I could have my proverbial cake and eat it too.

Sogang is a reputable Jesuit university, one of the top-tier universities in South Korea. The quality of education is high and for many years, it has been one of the go-to universities for foreigners who want to study in South Korea. Since 2004, the number of exchange students and foreign student enrollment has steadily increased. When I first applied for graduate school, the university had begun providing full scholarships to non-Korean citizens wanting to enroll. This was one of the determining factors for choosing Sogang University because tuition is not cheap in South Korea though it may cost a lot less than in the United States. I recommend that anyone planning to study in South Korea research the options for funding provided by the university or the Korean government, such as NIIED (The National Institute for International Education), which runs the Global Korea Scholarship. Be aware that some programs may require language training before regular classes may be taken and passing a Korean/ foreign language exam may be required as well to graduate.

I was accepted into the Department of English Language and Literature program. Classes at the graduate level were very different from undergraduate lectures. They were much smaller in size and much more interactive. To my advantage, (and possible detriment to my Korean) most classes were in English. Most of the Korean professors would conduct their classes in English, which was fortunate as academic Korean at the graduate level is extremely difficult. I took a couple of classes that were held in Korean, and it was only by the grace of the fact that papers had to be written in English that I managed to receive decent grades in those classes. I cannot stress enough how important language proficiency is when it comes to studying in Korea.

My (slowly degrading) Korean skills helped me land a job as a teacher's assistant (TA) within the department, a pretty good gig considering the hours and the workload. This allowed me to sustain a decent life for a grad student. I did not need to tutor on the side for extra income although the working hours allowed me to do that. Instead, I chose to spend that extra time on my studies as there was a lot for me to read up on. Being a TA in Korea is different from the United States, where you have teaching responsibilities.

In Korea, the TA's job is uncomplicated--performing tasks such as conveying information to/and from the administration, other departments, or within the department; making photocopies, and other miscellaneous chores. It is a great job for grad students. I was fortunate enough to work as a TA during the years of coursework for my master's and my Ph.D., which I finally completed in 2019. The coursework for a master's degree in Korea generally takes two years and a master's thesis. For a Ph.D., the allotted time to complete the degree is ten years, which includes two years of coursework. If you need more time, it is usually possible to extend the deadline for your dissertation, as it was in my case.

Life is a series of choices that you make. Some people make them early, planning their trajectory because they already know or have an idea which direction to go. Others, like me, make them as they present themselves. My story shows that you don't have to have a plan to make it in Korea, but you do need to create the momentum for opportunities to arise by experiencing, exploring, and productively engaging with the community and people around you. Learning Korean is a great start, even now as Koreans are getting better at English. As the church, Korean language classes are good places to make new friends, which may give rise to new opportunities that may take you to places you never dreamed of.

Living My Dream in Korea and How I Did It

By Ji-young Noh

The busy hum of voices filled the air. I reached for a basket of vibrant red apples at a local produce stand in Seongnam, South Korea. Inspired by the beautiful weather, I knew it would be a great day to explore. Judging by a large number of customers also searching for fruits and vegetables, I had made the right choice. Too many people passed by, this moment was just one of many in an ordinary day. For me, moments like these filled me with gratitude, contentment, and disbelief. Five years ago, this mundane scene was nothing more than an unimaginable and unattainable dream.

In 2016, I returned to Korea, my mother country for the first time since my adoption. I had the privilege of going on a motherland tour of South Korea. During the Holt Motherland tour in 2016. I had the opportunity to meet and share adoption stories with fellow adoptees. Although we came from different walks of life, we also shared a lot of similarities. The most prevalent similarity centered on our ethnicity and the loneliness we felt growing up in America. As I listened to each person's story, I began to feel less isolated. For the first time in my life, I felt like I was part of a community.

Ji-young Noh, photo courtesy of Ji-young Noh

Upon returning to the U.S., I felt like a different person. I began to question everything I thought I knew to be true. Throughout my childhood, my adoptive mother told me that South Korea was a very poor country. She said that Korean parents would discard their unwanted children in the garbage if they were born disabled like me. My adoptive mother told me that my Korean parents had given me up for adoption because I was born with cerebral palsy. At the time of my birth, my birth family was enduring financial hardship. My birth was an unwelcome mistake because of my cerebral palsy. My very existence had brought shame and dishonor upon my Korean family.

Despite what I was told as a child, I have always wanted to live in South Korea. Like many adopted children, I always wondered what it would be like to be born into a family and/or society where I looked like everyone else. I hated being "different." Unfortunately, I never felt like I belonged anywhere until I returned to Korea. People have asked why I decided to move here. I think it is because I wanted to explore my ethnic roots. I wanted to see what it feels like to live in the country where I belong.

In 2018, after visiting my mother country three times, I decided that I had to pursue my ultimate dream of living in Korea. After each visit, returning to America felt as if I was being taken back in chains against my will. My third visit and departure from Korea were the hardest. I still remember crying in the airport as I waited for my flight back to the States. Soon after that trip, I knew I had to abandon my comfort zone, and I started planning my big move.

To hold myself accountable, one of the first things I did was set a target date. After that, I purchased a one-way plane ticket. Given my unique challenges, I knew how important it was to be as financially and physically prepared as possible. I began by creating a budget for my first year in South Korea. Once I had paid for my plane ticket, I still needed enough money to maintain the cost of living in South Korea until I found gainful employment. Creating a financial plan gave me peace of mind. I had an estimate and a goal for how much I needed to save before leaving America.

The question of housing was also a concern. Unfortunately, Seoul is not as wheelchair accessible as the U.S., so I wanted to secure housing before my move. I knew that it would be extremely difficult to find housing that was not only wheelchair-accessible but also within my budget. It took me about six months, but I finally found a share house manager that would rent to me despite my physical challenges.

Next, I purchased a portable electric wheelchair online. My current wheelchair was way too heavy for me to lift by myself. In case of an emergency, I needed a wheelchair that was light enough for me to push or lift by myself. After purchasing the new chair, I donated my old one.

In the ten months leading up to my departure, I felt like I was riding a never-ending emotional roller coaster. I couldn't wait for my adventure to begin. I felt like a kid impatiently waiting to open my gifts on Christmas morning. At the same time, my uncertain future terrified me. There were countless times when I doubted my decision. I remember thinking, "What if I fail? What if I end up broke, hungry, and homeless in Korea? What if everyone's right, and I can't cut it after all?"

I'm not sure, but I probably drove my friends and family crazy with my incessant self-doubt. I feel very grateful and blessed to have had the continuous love, support, and encouragement of my friends and family, then and now.

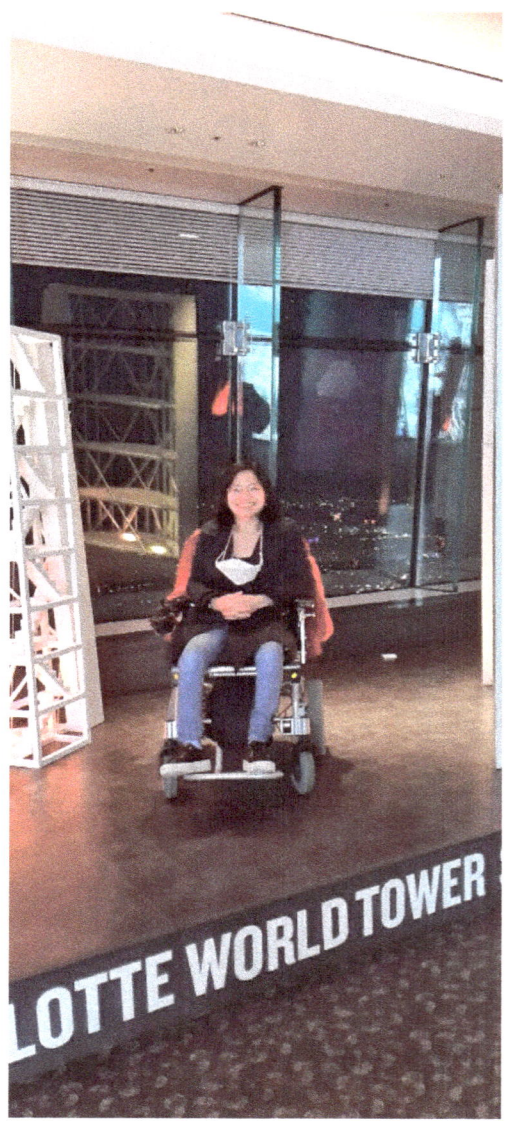

Ji-young Noh, photo courtesy of Ji-young Noh

My new life in Seoul, South Korea, began on July 3, 2019. Living here has been a mind-boggling, challenging, and humbling learning experience. Regardless, I would not change a minute of it. With the generosity of Global Overseas Adoptee Link (G.O.A.'L.), National Rights for the Child. (NCRC), and the Women's Disability Empathy (WDE) organization I was able to accomplish several of my goals during the first year. Within the first year in Korea, I wanted to recover my Korean citizenship, locate permanent housing, purchase a new electric wheelchair, start learning Korean and acquire financial assistance via the Korean government until I was able to secure gainful employment.

Shortly after my arrival, I decided to regain my Korean citizenship. I contacted the wonderful staff at Global Overseas Adoptee Link. (G.O.A.'L.). they guided me through the application process and translated my Korean citizenship application/documentation from English to Korean.

I received Korean language scholarships from both G.O.A.'L. and NCRC. Throughout the COVID-19 pandemic, both organizations provided adoptees living in Seoul with emergency relief kits composed of food and other daily living necessities. After regaining my Korean citizenship, I received guidance from a Korean organization called WDE. They guided me through the process of applying for Basic Living and Disability pension benefits. Currently, they are helping me obtain a new electric wheelchair, better suited for life in Korea.

Moving to Korea has been a cultural eye-opener. When I first moved here, I couldn't help but notice that Koreans avoided the rain. At first, I didn't understand why they used an umbrella every time it rained. One day curiosity got the best of me, and I decided to ask someone about it. The answer I got was simple. Korean people do not like to get wet. I think it is because the rain is dirty. There is a lot of pollution, especially in the larger cities.

Ji-young Noh, photo courtesy of Ji-young Noh

I also didn't understand why in Seoul they park their cars on the sidewalk. Even now I still find myself getting frustrated and baffled by this. This is particularly challenging for someone in a wheelchair. Often the curb cutouts are blocked. This makes it more difficult to either get on the sidewalk or navigate my wheelchair around the vehicles. Fortunately, I have become more comfortable driving my wheelchair in the side streets and alleyways. I am also surprised by the number of buildings that have stairs leading to the elevator. In my opinion, it makes more sense to remove the stairs after installing the elevator. Isn't that the whole purpose of the elevator?

On a more positive note, there are many facets of Korean culture that I find refreshing and heartwarming. I'm still surprised by how safe South Korea is. If you accidentally leave your phone, purse, or wallet somewhere, (not always but oftentimes) it will still be there upon your return. If not, it's usually because someone turned it in to the proper authorities already.

One day when my friend and I were hanging out together in Seoul, I lost my wallet in a crowded subway station. By the time I realized that it was missing, we had already left the station. I immediately panicked because my "entire life" was in that wallet. My friend and I retraced our steps, but unfortunately, we couldn't find it.

If I'd lost my wallet in the United States, I would have had to immediately call and cancel my bank cards. However, in Korea my language barrier complicates things. Since I didn't know what else to do, I called 112. English speakers can call this number if they need to contact the police. Unlike me, my friend speaks Korean very well. Thankfully, she was able to tell the police officers what happened. The responding officers contacted the police department inside the subway where I'd lost my wallet. Someone had already found my wallet and turned it in, they were just waiting for me to get it. I was relieved to find that none of my belongings were missing. If this had happened in America, the outcome may have been quite different.

I have heard people say that Koreans seem aloof and less welcoming. I do not find this to be true. For example, I have always been directionally challenged. I tend to get lost very easily especially in unfamiliar places. In South Korea, every time I ask for directions there is always someone willing to help. Some people have even taken me to the location themselves. Perhaps people are kind to me because of my language barrier, or my disability. Regardless, I have found most Koreans to be kind and helpful.

This journey has taught me a lot about myself and the world around me. The past couple of years has shown me that any dream, no matter how big or small, may be realized. I know that this will sound cliché, but in my experience, if you work hard and never give up on your dream, anything is possible.

I admit there have been times when I not only doubted myself but also my decision to continue living in South Korea. Thoughts of self-doubt usually present themselves when I am attempting to read, write, or converse with someone in Korean. Sometimes I wish I could just learn the Korean language overnight. It would be nice to be able to communicate in my original mother tongue without dying of embarrassment. However, if this experience has taught me anything, it's the importance of having patience with oneself. We are often kind, patient, and understanding toward others, but we forget to do the same for ourselves. Despite all the challenges, I know I made the right decision to follow my dreams. I have a bad habit of living my life solely by what seems logical. I have come to realize that although logic is important, I also must follow my heart.

It has been my honor and privilege to share my story with you. I hope that my story will inspire others to follow their dreams no matter how unrealistic they may seem. Please remember that your dreams and aspirations do not have to make sense to other people. They just must make sense to you. Of course, there will be many challenges along the way, but never give up on your dream. In life we have three choices: we may give in, give up, or fight for want we want. The choice is up to you, but I hope that you will choose the latter because you deserve the best that life has to offer.

Korea Story

By Scott Kaveny

This is the story about my adoption and how I came to find my birth family. I'm a 37-year-old athlete living in Park City, Utah in the United States. I was adopted into an Irish-American family at three months old with my twin brother, Kelly. Originally, I wanted to go to Korea to obtain dual citizenship for my sport as a freestyle skier. Korean Citizenship ended up being more work than I thought.

It all started one summer night in 2014 when I was still living in Colorado. On August 6th I was driving to Park City, Utah to ski jump. My best friend and second father, Clyde Getty, who was a two-time Olympic freestyle skier in his 50's at the time, encouraged me to get dual citizenship if I wanted to be in the Olympics and to move to Utah. Mind you, I was only seven years into my career in freestyle skiing. Even though at the time, I was over-medicated, tired, depressed, and overweight, I still had a lot of athletic ability, and I had a dream. That six-hour conversation planted a seed within me that changed my life. I took his advice and moved out to Utah later that year.

Scott Kaveny, photo courtesy of Scott Kaveny

After I settled in, I joined the Park City Freestyle Ski Team. However, I faced numerous challenges. This move cost me everything. By the middle of that year, I was homeless, jobless, and had an injury on my left ACL from my last competition that February.

Fortunately, there was a group of people that took me under their wing and helped me enroll in a personal development program. I started to heal emotionally and mentally. In times past, I never had the permission to speak up or to follow my dreams wholeheartedly due to a very controlling family dynamic. It was nobody's fault: it was just the way it was. I spent the next few years in this program investing in myself instilling new habits and ways of thinking. After three long years of personal, emotional, and mental healing, I graduated in late 2017. I started to get back into skiing and began thinking about what Clyde said about dual citizenship back in 2014.

I called the adoption agency in Greeley, Colorado, and found that they had my adoption papers from when I arrived from Korea with Kelly. I requested a copy of my adoption records and received them around the beginning of November. Once I was able to see them, I was able to learn more details about my twin brother and myself and our flight from Korea to Colorado where our adoptive family lived. I was also able to find out more from when I was three months old up to about one year old, like my personality, what I liked and disliked, etc.

This was very insightful information to finally have, and it helped me emotionally realize how much my adoptive family has always loved me and did their best as parents. I also knew that this was the tip of a very big iceberg. I wanted to go to South Korea and find our birth family. But I felt stuck and a little overwhelmed by this new information. It did not help that I was also struggling financially.

It wasn't until the summer of 2019, as I was water ramping (ski jumping) in with my team, that I had the reminder I needed from Jeff Yingling, the temporary head coach for Park City Freestyle Ski Team. He again encouraged me to get dual citizenship, as it would allow me to compete in the World Cup. I started to research organizations that would help me with this process in Korea. Thus began another step and process.

According to the papers that I received in 2018, I found that only my birth mother's name was on my birth certificate and that my adoption agency was called Eastern Social Welfare Society. I googled to see if I could find a place that would help me with this little bit of information and found an organization called G.O.A.'L. They helped me get the information I needed to find my birth family and to obtain dual citizenship. I corresponded with them from the summer of 2019 through the summer of 2020. This was when I started to dream again and realize that I could make this real.

2020 and the COVID-19 pandemic caused a lot of chaos for me. I moved three times that year to different rooms-for-rent within Utah. I had to rebook my Korea trip seven times due to COVID-19 restrictions and cancelations. I was also transitioning from my job to growing my own business. Through all this, I never gave up on my dream, and on June 4, 2020, I was finally able to put money down for my trip to South Korea. Regardless of what the media or what my friends said, I needed to follow my heart.

During this time, G.O.A.'L. helped me find the resources and collect the paperwork I needed to travel from the United States to South Korea. That particular time was not easy. The whole process of dual citizenship and finding my birth family was so alien to me. My friends Eirik and Joohoon helped me immensely throughout that time.

Toward the end of September 2020, my booking stabilized finally with the Lufthansa airline. Despite all the moves and travel cancelations, I made because of COVID, I held on, and was able to hop onto my flight for South Korea on October 5, 2020.

When I got there on October 6th, I found that my Airbnb quarantine room previously arranged was no longer valid or available. I was forced to move to a hotel that was set up as an official quarantine facility for foreigners. I ended up staying at Marina Bay for two weeks. This was quite a financial strain. I also had another problem; I was running out of money. My business had been faltering since the beginning of September 2020. I barely had enough money for that quarantine facility for two weeks. I was not sure how I would obtain more money to stay in South Korea for the rest of the trip. Although my stay at Marina Bay was great, the financial pressure was challenging.

When I got to Korea, Eirik helped me find economical accommodations for the next two months. It was a guesthouse for adult adoptees called Koroot run by Pastor Kong and Chris Kim, who were very helpful. They mapped out Seoul for me and I was able to explore the city. Simultaneously, I was talking to Bang, a caseworker at Eastern Social Welfare Society who was able to eventually locate my birth family. It was easier to do because I was a twin. I later learned that Korean adoptees between 1982 and 1984 had tremendous issues with their records because of government re-organization and allowing more adoptions than ever.

Scott Kaveny, photo courtesy of Scott Kaveny

I felt like this was meant to be. I moved out of Koroot and decided to move to Myeongdong and do more of my exploring and business rebuilding there. It was at this time I met John Tae Shik Ha through G.O.A.'L. He was invaluable in helping me to figure out what my next steps were towards dual citizenship and a reunion with my birth family.

183

I also got to know him personally, and he has helped me grow my business and contributed to some of my YouTube video blogs (vlogs).

On November 9, 2020, Bang told me that my birth mother responded, and she was crying on the phone with the belief that my twin and I were dead since birth. Once she then realized that we were both alive, she was very grateful that I sought her out. Bang helped set up a time to meet on November 12, 2020.

This was a very magical time. I was able to discover that my twin and I had an older brother, Jong-gak, and a younger brother, So-Young. We will all get together at some point. Three days after I met my birth family, my mother offered a place for me to stay at her home in Ilsan, and that is when I stayed for another month and got to know my family. Obtaining my dual citizenship also went very well. Joohoon helped me find the resources, the facilities, and the papers I needed to be translated so everything may be finalized when I fly back to South Korea in the spring of 2023. I submitted my papers three days before I left on December 15, 2020. In the meantime, my birth family and I, as well as my twin brother, have all been keeping in touch via text, FaceTime, and recorded video. I've been trying to learn Korean as well since I came back to the States.

I'm so grateful for all that has happened and hope it can inspire other adoptees. Never give up no matter how hard the journey is to find your birth family or to obtain dual citizenship. Just because I'm fortunate enough to have found my birth family does not mean that the journey was easy. It was among the hardest things I've ever had to do in my life. Not to mention learning to embrace where I was born. 2018 was the first year I started to open up to this fact. But looking back: it was so worth it. With a lot of willpower, persistence, and faith, you can accomplish anything.

A Swedish Adoptee Story

By LiMarie Eunmi Andersson

My Korean name is Eunmi Oh (오은미) and I was born in 1980 in Gimje, a small town in Korea. (My adoption papers state that I was born in Seoul.)

I was adopted to Sweden at the age of 11 months. Before that, I lived with 2 different foster families in Korea. In Sweden, I grew up in a small community, together with a sister one-year younger who is also adopted from South Korea.

The longing and desire to go to South Korea has existed off and on since my early childhood, as I also had free access to all adoption documents, that my Swedish parents had put in a folder.

"I have for a long time struggled with feelings and thoughts about and around happiness, my conclusion so far is that it is not the happiness itself I am yearning for, instead it is contentedness."

It was not until adulthood in 2013, that I decided to visit my motherland.

I went on a group trip called, "First Trip Home" with other adoptees from all over the world. The trip was organized by the organization G.O.A.'L. I also got help searching for my biological family.

That journey changed a lot of things for me; it changed me inside and out. I came there with a belief that I had built my life on a solid foundation, a foundation that carried my idea of how my adoption happened, how my biological family lived, what their circumstances were, and why I had been given up for adoption.

The foundation collapsed.

My adoption papers did not match in the way that the truth was folding out in front of me.

But the main thing that hit me very hard was that before I left South Korea at the age of 11 months, my biological parents had been looking for me. They had been told that I had already been adopted. And that it was too late to take me back.

185

After my first return to South Korea, I have been back almost every year.

In 2013, became self-aware of the unsaturated hunger within me, and of the desire to get to know my roots. A fire was lit inside of me, and I decided to take back everything that had been stolen from me through my adoption.

My goal, or rather my emotional goal of living in South Korea for a while, was to saturate my deep feelings of hunger.

I wanted to feel inner satisfying satiety, and also, I wished to experience the feeling of similar longing for my second home country, Sweden.

We, humans, become quite blind at home, so, in other words, I wanted the balance of my inner longing to attain a balance.

I wanted to give justice to both countries.

In a simplified conclusion, I wanted to experience with my senses the "typical" Korean experience, and "check" it off my heavy emotional list, so I could say to myself, "Finally, I've seen it!" South Korea to Sweden, one to one.

With the trip, I wanted to dive deep. I wanted to jump. I wanted to fall, with the goal in sight with a satisfyingly warm set of satisfaction.

As a mother, it was also important to me that my children should be able to share the experience of the South Korean heritage because it was also something that belongs to them.

LiMarie Eunmi Andersson, photo courtesy of LiMarie Eunmi Andersson

I wanted to give them, albeit, an unconscious image of belonging, where they could feel that they do not look distinctly different. A kind of understanding that something that may be different in Swedish terms can be something rich and beautiful in other eyes. I mean many things not only physical attributes.

In July 2020, I went with my family (partner and three youngest children born in the years 2008, 2010, and 2012, and our dog) to South Korea to stay, with an undeclared home date.

There was an incredible amount of planning and arrangement behind it… and to do it in the middle of an insistent pandemic did not make it easier. Since South Korea had withdrawn the tourist visa, we had to apply for an F4 Visa.

We end up staying for nine months. We struggled from the beginning, partly with the obligatory supervised quarantine, then I had a hospital stay with two of the kids for two weeks due to COVID-19. Not being able to make myself understood made me feel exposed and without control of the situation.

Nothing turned out as we had imagined. We lived in three different places in South Korea: the first place was a penthouse, with incredibly keen walls, where we did not dare to move even barely due to the ajumma, who was disturbed by the children's play. The other place was a smaller two-bedroom apartment, with windows against another apartment wall and full of damp air and spiders, which woke us up at night. In that apartment, I also had several supernatural experiences, which led to my Korean mother bringing a monk to clean the apartment from negative energies, but I only experienced a marginal difference.

The lesson though brought me and my mother closer together as it confirmed an invisible bond that we share about being able to see and feel the non-physical world.

Another experience with an inference is not to entrust anyone, not even "friends" with something that can put you in a vulnerable position, when you are in such a vulnerable place, as in a new and relatively unknown country.

I'm talking about a significant amount of money but also help with interpretation and other omissions that can be distorted and embezzled.

I just want to write this as a word of warning.

LiMarie Eunmi Andersson, photo courtesy of LiMarie Eunmi Andersson

We experienced awful things because of a couple that we trusted, and they deceived us badly.

This made us decide to move again for the third time to a completely different city in South Korea.

My Korean brother helped us move this third and final time to an apartment that was beyond our expectations. We felt safe there, with guards and with cameras and code locks. It was a newly built nice and super modern apartment.

Moving to Korea is very well organized and efficient. You contact a moving company, and they can help you pack your things for you, they can unpack things for you, and they take care of the entire movie, of course for a fee. But it is relatively low compared to what the price is in Sweden for the same thing.

We moved to the fourth floor in a 23-floor building.

They use high cranes on the truck to move everything through a window. Everything with the move was finished in one day.

It was when we got to the last apartment that we felt safe, and we could start our life in Korea.

We started with language lessons, and we set up with everyday chores that we might otherwise take for granted, like decorating the apartment, bank matters, paying bills, riding the local bus, and botanizing among shops and the market. We had a lot of help from different language translation apps. Of course, sometimes it will turn out with incorrect answers.

You learn how to not look at it deadly seriously, at least like this afterward.

We met my Korean family a few times. Due to the corona, we could not meet as often as we wanted. But just the certainty of knowing that they lived close was more than enough for me. My sister lived within walking distance, and I could happily just walk away to say hello to her children.

Now in retrospect, that feeling of certainty of their presence felt incredibly healing to me.

During the day, the children had their Swedish school online.

Where we first lived, the children started school in a native Korean school where they learned Korean and the Korean alphabet. The teachers were incredibly helpful, and they could make themselves understood by English. The children went three days a week divided by age and grade to minimize the number of children being in school at the same time.

My youngest became incredibly welcomed, she received drawings, notes in English, and sweet gifts from her classmates. Her teacher was amazing!

The other teachers were also good and made sure that the children enjoyed themselves.

When you have three children, you do know that they are all individuals and function differently even if they are siblings; they all have different conclusions of the same experience of their time in a Korean school.

In the native Korean school, the language barrier was still the biggest challenge and stressful for all of us. My advice is to go on your gut feeling as a parent, be persistent, and communicate daily with the teachers.

Now, when I am thinking back, I pat myself on my shoulder!

As a Swedish parent, you have a lot to say about your children in a Swedish school.

Someone who does not have children of his own told me that you do not have the same say in a Korean school, but my experience still says that your parents' authority is not ignored.

Reflections:

Sweden is different in many ways from Korea; I have felt the differences through culture clashes many times. Sweden has come a long way in gender equality and is seen as a role model for many countries.

Korean society, on the other hand, is patriarchally and hierarchically structured. I am used to being able to carry my bag, to open the door myself, to defend myself, and be able to speak for myself. There is a kind of tiger in me that can roar when I feel too depressed, and I'm proud of it.

What I have not figured out is if it comes from my upbringing in Sweden or my Korean mother.

Maybe it's kind of a combination of everything.

As a Korean adoptee in Korea, you assimilate well, but it was obvious that it seems hard for many natives to understand why I could not speak Korean because they can see that I am Korean ... this creates frustration inside me: The feeling of not belonging even in my birth country.

I understand it is a common feeling to experience among adoptees.

It can be frustrating to not have anyone to lean on if you stay in South Korea for a longer period. As for us, we had no safety net here, often we felt like some disguised aliens since all of us looked Asian.

However, I have had incredibly nice friends who helped me translate online in certain situations when I needed help, even though by a different time zone.

But as for interpretation I know several organizations offer help with that. Including Adoptee Hub.

Now back in Sweden, I have had a ton of experiences. Many of them I would have rather not had at all, and it is part of the package from this experience.

I am proud that despite many setbacks, I have given my children a life experience that they will carry with them for the rest of their life. I am so grateful that I have been able to give them a tool, built on knowledge gained from their own experiences, to be able to choose their own choices in life regarding their Korean heritage, something that many of us adoptees hunger to experience and should have the right to do.

Journal / Notes

Helpful Korean Words & Phrases

English	Korean	Phonetic
Hello!	안녕하세요!	An-nyeong-ha-se-yo!
My name is _____.	제 이름은 _____.	Jeh ee-reum-un _____.
Answering the phone; equivalent to "Hello?"	여보세요?	Yeo-bo-se-yo?
Please give me this.	이거 주세요	Ee-guh juh-say-yo
Do you have this?	이것이세요?	Igeos-iseyo?
I don't have this.	이것없어	Igeo eobs-eo
Excuse me but... (getting a server's attention at a restaurant)	저기요...	Chogiyo...
Yes/I agree.	네; 맞아요	Nae; ma-ja-yo
No.	아니요	Ah-ni-yo
Where is the toilet? (Do not use the word bathroom)	화장실이 어디예요?	Hwa-jang-shil-ee udee-ye-yo?
How much is it?	얼마에요?	Uhl-mah-eh-yo?
Telling a taxi driver to "go there"	가주세요	Gaseyo
Nice to meet you.	반갑습니다	Ban-gap-sum-ni-da

English	Korean	Phonetic
How are you?	잘 지내셨어요?	Jal-ji-nae-syut-eo-yo?
I will start eating; bon appetite!	잘 먹겠습니다!	Jal meok-ge-sseum-ni-da!
The meal was good.	잘 먹었습니다	Jal meo-geo-sseum-ni-da
You can do it! Or "Good luck!"	화이팅	Hwa-it-ting
Goodbye! (informal)	안녕	Ahn-nyung!
Goodbye (formal) When you are leaving	안녕히 계세요	Ahn-nyung-hee geh-seh-yo
Goodbye (formal) When a person is leaving.	안녕히 가세요	Ahn-nyung-hee gah-seh-yo
I'm lost.	길을 잃었어요	Gil-eul ilh-uht-suh-yo
I don't speak Korean well.	한국말 잘 못해요	Hahn-guhk-mal jal moht-heh-yo
Do you speak English?	영어 할 수 있어요?	Yung-uh hal su-eet-suh-yo?
Please speak slowly	천천히 말씀해 주세요	Chun-chun-hee mal-sseum-heh ju-seh-yo
I am not feeling well.	몸이 안 좋아요	Mohm-yi-ahn-jo-a-yo
Where is the pharmacy?	약국이 어디인가요?	Yak-kuk-yi-eo-di-in-ga-yo?

English	Korean	Phonetic
Where is the bank?	은행 어디있나요?	Eun-hang-eo-di-it-na-yo?
The food was so good!	맛있어요!	Mat-it-uh-yo
I am full.	배불러요	Bae-bul-leo-yo
It's okay.	괜찮아요	Gyeon-chan-a-yo
Excuse me! (To get attention)	잠깐만요 저기요	Jam-ggan-mahn-yo Jam-ggan-mahn-yo
It's too expensive.	너무 비싸요.	Neo-mu-bi-ssa-yo
What is this?	이게 뭔가요?	Yi-gae-mon-ga-yo?
Where is the ATM?	현금 인출기 어디있나요?	Hyun-geum-in-chul-gi-eo-di-it-na-yo?
Thank you for all your hard work. (This will garner a lot of respect from Koreans.)	수고했어요	Sugohaess-eoyo